THREE DIMENSIONAL GRAPHICS

Edited by KEIZO MATSUI

RIKUYO-SHA

THREE
DIMENSIONAL
GRAPHICS

松井桂三編

六耀社

Introductory Remarks　凡例

PL	Planner	プランナー
PR	Producer	プロデューサー
CD	Creative Director	クリエイティブ・ディレクター
AD	Art Director	アートディレクター
DE	Designer	デザイナー
CN	Construction	構造デザイン
WR	Copywriter	コピーライター
IL	Illustrator	イラストレーター
PH	Photographer	カメラマン
MA	Manufacturer	製作者
AG	Agency	エージェント
CL	Client	クライアント

CONTENTS
目次

6
INTRODUCTION
Emilio Ambasz
・
序文
エミリオ・アンバース

11
DIRECT MAILS
INVITATIONS
ANNOUNCEMENTS
・
ダイレクトメール
招待状
案内状

69
CHRISTMAS AND NEW YEAR'S CARDS
BIRTHDAY CARDS
OTHER GREETING CARDS
・
クリスマスカード
年賀状
バースデーカード
グリーティングカード

117
POSTERS
CALENDARS
PACKAGING
CATALOGUES
MAGAZINE INSERT
P.O.P. TOOLS
ILLUSTRATIONS
・
ポスター
カレンダー
パッケージ
カタログ
雑誌折込広告
P.O.P.ツール
イラストレーション

154
THREE-DIMENSIONAL GREETING CARDS
AND DIRECT MAILS IN THE UNITED STATES
Shin'ichiro Tora
・
アメリカにおける3DのカードとDM
虎 新一郎

158
PROFILE
・
作家プロフィール

私のデザインワーク
エミリオ・アンバース

私はグラフィック・デザインを専門としているわけではない。もともとプロダクトや建物など〈モノ〉を作るのが本業で、そのうちのいくつかに、たまたま紙という材料を用いたということなのである。もちろん、たまにグラフィック・シンボル（タクシー展のロゴタイプ）やカード（ブリュッセル・ランベール銀行他）を考案したり、ポスターのレイアウト（ゲイジー他）をしたりもするが、そのような時も印刷物というよりは三次元のオブジェとしてとらえている。そうするのは、多分、私がモノの中にある生命のようなものに魅せられているからだと思う。私には2枚の紙の間に生じるごく僅かな空間や、二つのファサードの内にとじ込められたマッスとみなされる紙の厚さに対して、シュールレアリスト的妄想をもっている。こうしてみると、紙というのは二つの特性をもった構築性のある材料に思えてくる。それは、その背後にあるものを暗示させる保護膜であり、同時に、デザインがその中に入り込めるほどのソフトな容積のあるものである。

私のデザイン・アプローチには二つの明確な姿勢がある。一つは、いつもうまくいくとは限らないが、仕事をこなすにあたって先を見越したデザインを考えること、もう一つは身のまわりにあるものの再利用を考える、ということである。

第1の例として、カレンダー・メモリー・バッグがある。これはもちろんカレンダーとして使える（ただし、忘れてしまいたいような厭な日を破りとっても、その月全体の構造は変わらないままであるという点が、他のカレンダーとは違う）。しかし、私にとって紙というものは内部空間をもったものであるから、料理法のメモ、新聞の切り抜き、クリーニング屋の預り証や宝くじ、赤ちゃんのスナップ写真、落葉など、誰もがとっておきたいと思うようなものを入れておけるようなカレンダーを考案した。カレンダーは来るべきこと（l'avenir）を計画するだけでなく、長くとどめておきたい過去の断片（le souvenir）の数々をしまっておくという役目をもつべきだと信じているからである。

第2の点だが、私は生まれつき怠慢なせいか、身辺を見渡して、新しい素材よりむしろすでにあるもので何か再利用できるものはないか探し求める（先にあげたカレンダーは、会社の大型封筒と食料雑貨店のクラフト紙の袋を使った）。

しかし、このような私の姿勢は、進歩を盲目的に信奉し、新製品は人類の抱える問題に解決を与えるものであると信じきってきた先達を裏切るような後ろめたさを少なからず感じるので、それを釈明すべく、私なりの哲学を開陳する必要があるかもしれない。それは、概ね、次のようなものである。

〈ヨーロッパが永遠に追求するものはユートピア、終着点としての理想郷であり、アメリカが回帰するのはアルカデ

ィア、始まりとしての田園の理想郷である。昔ながらのアルカディアの像はヒューマニズムの田園だが、アメリカはこれを人間の手になる人工の樹木と、心理的な影からなる森に転じてしまった。

周辺にある木を使った初期の椅子づくりのように、最近のアメリカのデザイナーの一部は、身辺にある製品や製造工程（時には、記憶さえも）を利用し始めた。しかし、もはや木はなく、残っているのは椅子ばかりという状態であるから、デザイナーたるもの、自分の創るものが元の状態に戻せるか、あるいは再利用できるものか、心して仕事をしなければならない。そうでないと、自らつくった砂漠の庭師と成り果ててしまうかもしれない。昔から永遠に変わらない身振りで、奇術をあやつってきた集団であるデザイナーは、今、始まりの儀式のもち方を学ぶのとあわせて、終焉の儀式の段取りをも学ぶ必要がある。

このような秩序の考え方の底流にある原理は、オープン・エンディドシステムである。この原理によれば、各構成要素のアイデンティティーをぎりぎりにもちながら、それら要素間の相互関係のパターンは、変幻きわまりなく変化する。

私の仕事の方法論的原理は、原型を探り、パイロットとなる解答をまず求めて、それを一般的方法に公式化し、次の段階で特定の問題に対応する応用法を考えていくというものである。

絶えず生成の状態にある、人間のつくった自然とダイナミックに呼応するデザイン概念には、いくつかの特殊作業が含まれる。まず第1は、「経験的」なもので、人間がつくった田園に広まっている製品や製造技術の分布図をつくること、第2は「標準化」で、経験的手法や製品の分布図の活用をはかるため、個人のニーズや願望のプログラムを、より大きな社会全体の必要という文脈で展開させること。第3は「総合的」作業で、人間の恐れや願望を、経験領域から強いられた限界や、標準規範的領域の重圧とうまく両立させることができるような新しい構造にカタチを与えることである。

デザイナーの真の仕事は、機能的ニーズや行動上のニーズが満たされた段階に始まると確信している。われわれは、人間の実用的なニーズを充足させることを願ってモノをつくっているわけではなく、むしろ、自らの内に沸き上がってくる情熱や想像力を満足させるためである。われわれを創造にかりたてるものは空腹ではなく、愛とか恐れ、時としては不思議と感じる心である。詩心といったものが、われわれのモノづくりの基礎にある。デザイナーを取り巻く環境は変わったかもしれない。しかし、《実用品に詩的なカタチを与える》その仕事は今も不変である、と私は考える。〉（原文は『グラフィック・デザイン』No.69, 1978による）

建築家／グラフィック＆インダストリアル・デザイナー

My Design Work
Emilio Ambasz

In truth, I do not make graphic designs. I am an object maker, whether products or buildings, and some of them just happen to be made of paper. Oh, well—yes—once in a while I create graphic symbols (like the taxi exhibition's logotype) and cards (like Banque Bruxelles Lambert one, etc.) or layout a poster (like the Geigy, Surface & Ornament one, etc.). But, even then, I must confess, I conceive them more as three-dimensional objects than as printing subjects. I do so, perhaps, because I am fascinated with the inner life of matter. I have a surrealist's obsession with both the infinitesimal space which occurs *between* two sheets of paper, and with the actual thickness of paper, which I perceive as a mass contained *within* two facades. Paper is then, for me, architectonic material with two attributes: it is a shield suggestive of that which is behind, and, at the same time, it is a volume, so soft that a design may dwell inside.

As for my attitude toward problem-solving in design, I can distinguish two features of my work. First, I try, not always successfully, to go beyond the problem-at-hand. Let us take for example the case of the calendar-memory bag. It can be used as a straightforward calendar (in that case it is like any other calendar, except for the possibility of tearing away any bad day which one may wish to forget, while still maintaining the month's overall structure). But since paper possesses for me an inner space, I have conceived this calendar so that one could keep within it those things one may wish to collect: recipes, newspaper clippings, laundry and lottery tickets, baby's snapshots, fallen leaves, etc. I believe that a calendar should help us plan not only for that which is to come (l'avenir), but it should also help us hold on to those instances of our past we may wish to keep (le souvenir).

The second characteristic of my approach to problem-solving is that, since I am so lazy, I always look around to see whether there is not something already existent which I may re-utilize. (In the calendar's case I re-utilized both inter-office envelopes and grocery brown-bags.)

Since I feel slightly guilty for having betrayed our forefathers' blind trust in progress, and their belief in new products as the healers of mankind's problems, I have felt compelled to develop a little philosophical theory to justify such behaviors. It goes, more or less, as follows:

"Europe's eternal quest remains Utopia, the myth of the end. America's returning myth is Arcadia, the eternal beginning. While the traditional vision of Arcadia is that of a humanistic garden, America's Arcadia has turned into a man-made nature, a forest of artificial trees and of mental shadows.

Like the first chair-maker who used the wood of surrounding trees, so are now some of America's designers beginning to use the objects and processes (and sometimes, the memories) surrounding them. But, since no more trees remain, just chairs, they have to be careful their creations are either capable of returning to their previous state, or of being re-utilized, lest they find themselves the gardeners of a man-made desert. The designer, that old thaumaturgus of the eternal gesture, must now learn both how to celebrate the ritual of the beginning and how to design for the ceremony of the end.

The principle underlying such notions of order is the concept of open-ended systems, where the possibilities for changing patterns of relationships remain always open, but where each of the component elements maintains its irreducible identity. The methodological principle guiding my work is to search for prototypical or pilot solutions which can first be formulated into a general method, and then applied to solve specific problems.

A notion of design in dynamic consonance with a man-made nature in a constant state of becoming involves specialized tasks. First, *empirical*, to construct a cartography of the products and production techniques which populate the man-made garden. Second, *normative*, to develop a program of individual needs and desires in the context of a larger program of social necessities, in order to guide the utilization of the empirical cartography. Third, *synthetic*, to give form to new structures which will allow man to reconcile his fears and desires with the limitations imposed by the empirical realm and the pressure of the normative domain.

I believe the designer's real task begins once functional and behavioral needs have been satisfied. We create objects not only because we hope to satisfy the pragmatic needs of man, but mainly because we need to satisfy the demands of our passions and imagination. It is not hunger, but love and fear, and sometimes wonder, which make us create. The poetic principle is the fundament of our creating objects. The designer's milieu may have changed but the task, I believe, remains the same: to give poetic form to the pragmatic." (from "Graphic Design No. 69")

Architect, Graphic and Industrial Designer

DIRECT MAILS
INVITATIONS
ANNOUNCEMENTS
・
ダイレクトメール
招待状
案内状

1

1・2

電話機/蓄音機、1986
AD　松井桂三
DE　松井桂三
CN　松井桂三、清水栄治
AG　松井桂三デザイン室
CL　ワールド
ファッションメーカーのマガジン「リベラリスト」の付録を兼ねたダイレクトメール。86年度ADC賞（東京）、ニューヨークADC受賞

1・2

Direct Mail, 1986
AD　Keizo Matsui
DE　Keizo Matsui
CN　Keizo Matsui
　　Eiji Shimizu
AG　Keizo Matsui and Associates
CL　World
A direct mail also serving as an extra of *Liberalist*, a magazine of a fashion manufacturer. Awarded Tokyo ADC Prize 1986, and Art Directors Club New York Award Winner.

3
ヒロココシノ
パリ・コレクション招待状, 1987
AD　松井桂三
DE　松井桂三
CN　松井桂三
AG　松井桂三デザイン室
CL　ヒロココシノ
　　インターナショナル
段ボール製のポストカードがそのまま招待状になっている。

3
Invitation to Paris Collection, 1987
AD　Keizo Matsui
DE　Keizo Matsui
CN　Keizo Matsui
AG　Keizo Matsui and Associates
CL　Hiroko Koshino International
An invitation postcard made of corrugated paper.

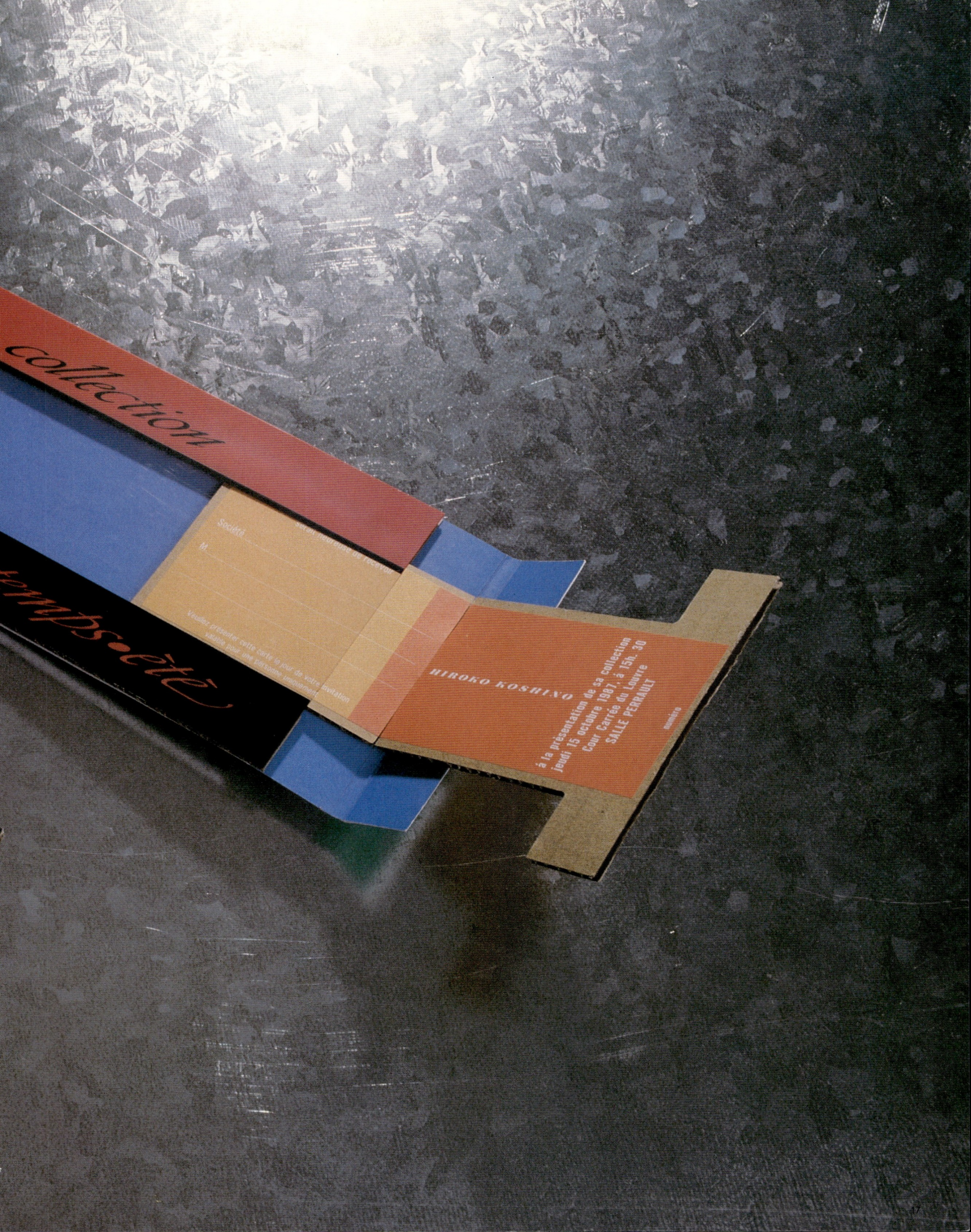

4
ヒロココシノ
パリ・コレクション招待状、1984
AD 松井桂三
DE 松井桂三
CN 松井桂三
AG 松井桂三デザイン室
CL ヒロココシノ
　　インターナショナル
ファッションショーの会場となるルーブル美術館中庭のテントを想定して制作された招待状。開くと、薄紙がふくらむ。

4
Invitation to Paris Collection, 1984
AD Keizo Matsui
DE Keizo Matsui
CN Keizo Matsui
AG Keizo Matsui and Associates
CL Hiroko Koshino International
An invitation letter in the image of the tent in the yard of Louvre Museum, the venue of the fashion show. The thin paper fills out when opened.

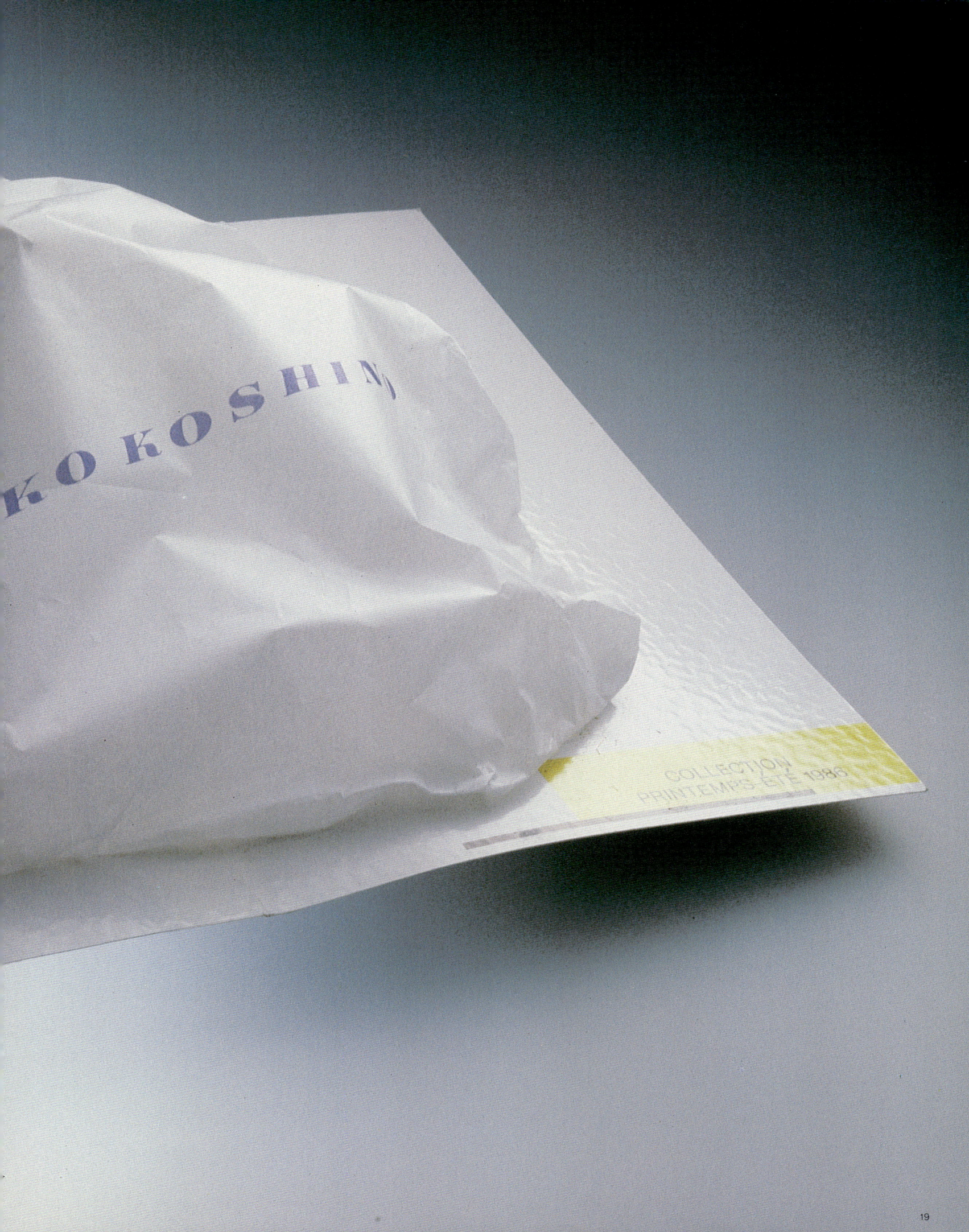

5	5
ヒロココシノ パリ・コレクション招待状、1986	Invitation to Paris Collection, 1986
AD 松井桂三	AD Keizo Matsui
DE 松井桂三	DE Keizo Matsui
CN 松井桂三、清水栄治	CN Keizo Matsui Eiji Shimizu
CL ヒロココシノ インターナショナル	CL Hiroko Koshino International
会場のテントをイメージ化した招待状	An invitation letter in the image of the tent for show

6
ヒロココシノ
パリ・コレクション案内状、1985
AD 松井桂三
DE 松井桂三
CN 松井桂三、清水栄治
CL ヒロココシノ
　　インターナショナル

6
Invitation to Paris Collection,
1985
AD Keizo Matsui
DE Keizo Matsui
CN Keizo Matsui
　　Eiji Shimizu
CL Hiroko Koshino
　　International

7

ヒロコオム ファッションショー
招待状、1986
AD　松井桂三
DE　松井桂三、清水栄治
CN　松井桂三、清水栄治
AG　松井桂三デザイン室
CL　ヒロココシノ
　　　インターナショナル
開くと、ラグビーボール形の立体
が現われる。

7

Invitation to Fashion Show, 1986
AD　Keizo Matsui
DE　Keizo Matsui
　　　Eiji Shimizu
CN　Keizo Matsui
　　　Eiji Shimizu
AG　Keizo Matsui and
　　　Associates
CL　Hiroko Koshino
　　　International
A decahedron in the image of a rugby ball comes out when opened.

8

ヒロココシノ
東京コレクション招待状、1984
AD 松井桂三
DE 松井桂三、長尾仁美
CL ヒロココシノ
　　インターナショナル

8

Invitation to Tokyo Collection,
1984
AD Keizo Matsui
DE Keizo Matsui
　　Hitomi Nagao
CL Hiroko Koshino
　　International

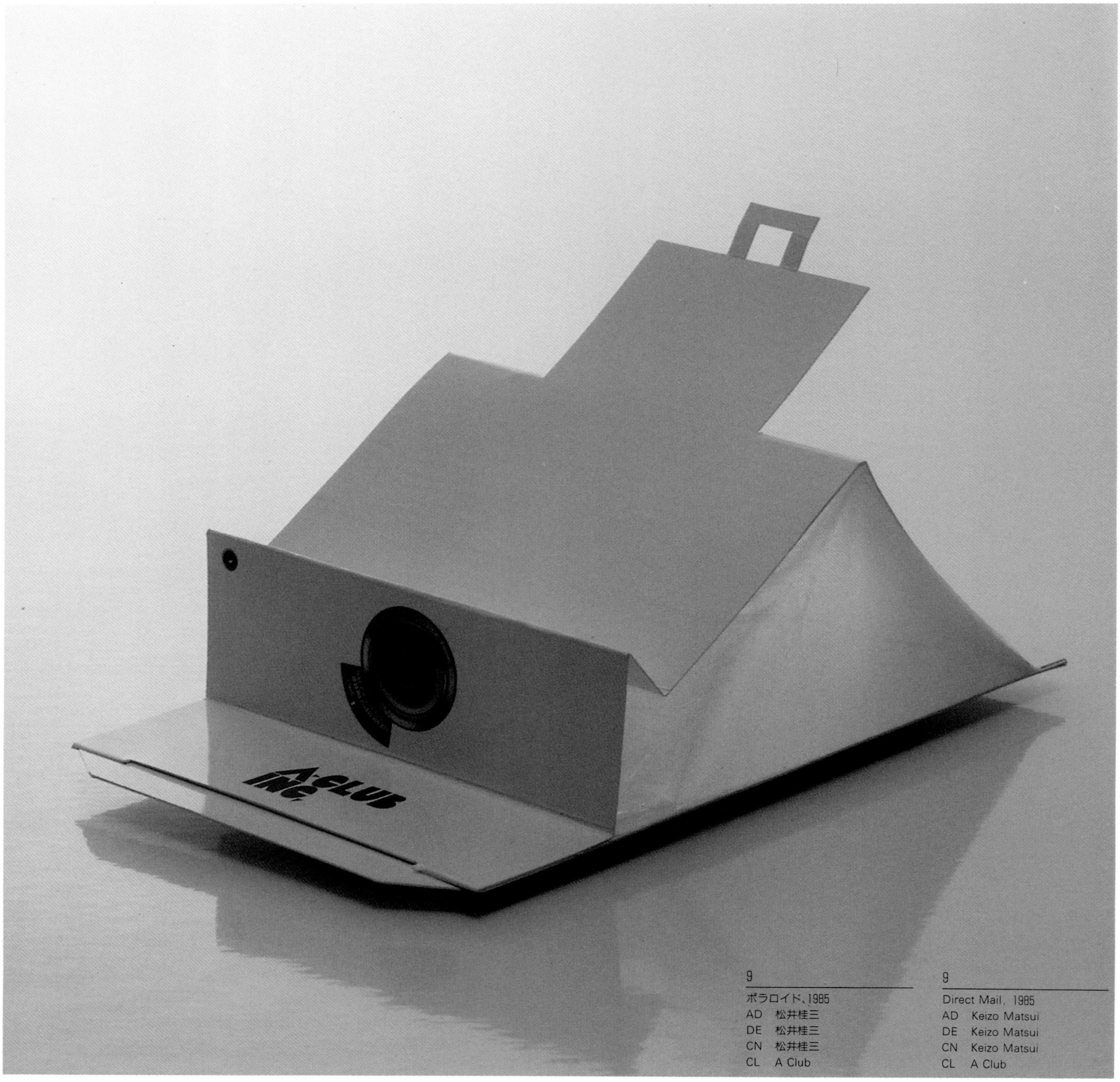

9
ポラロイド、1985
AD 松井桂三
DE 松井桂三
CN 松井桂三
CL A Club

9
Direct Mail, 1985
AD Keizo Matsui
DE Keizo Matsui
CN Keizo Matsui
CL A Club

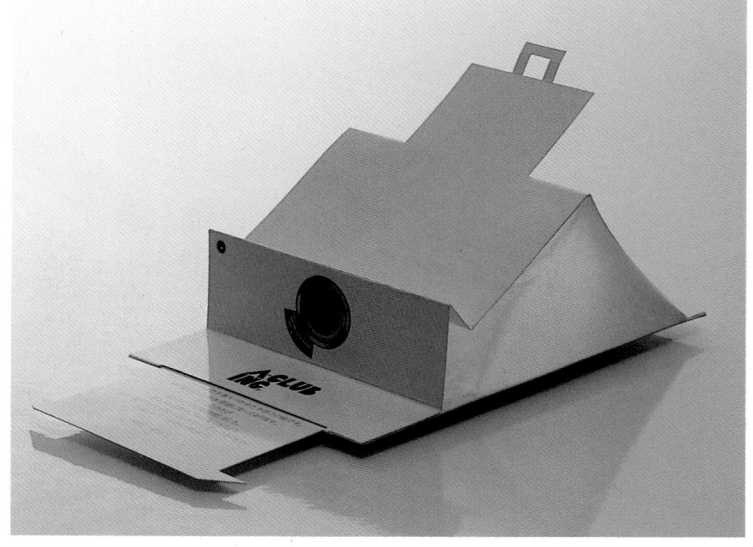

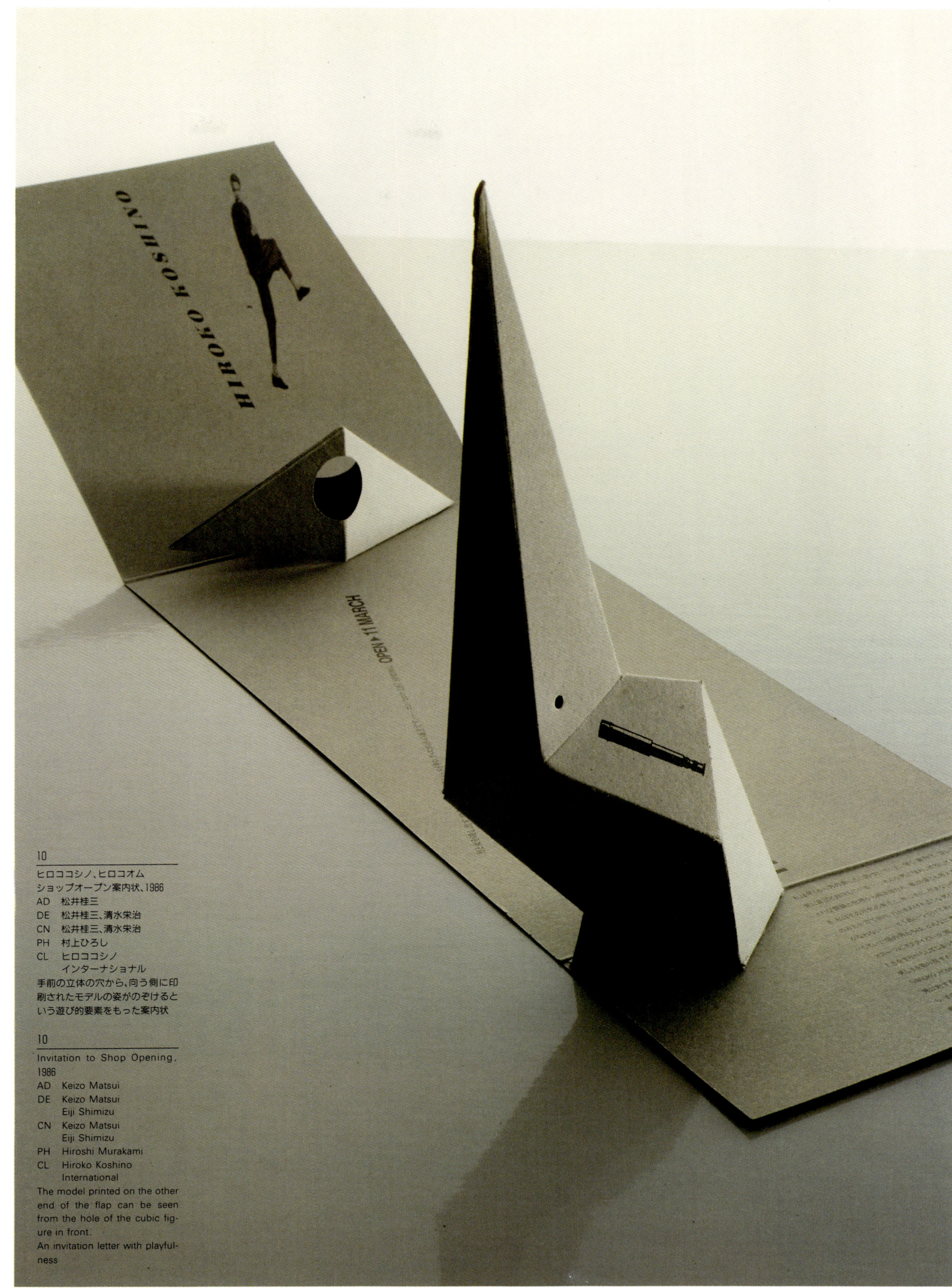

10
ヒロココシノ、ヒロコオム
ショップオープン案内状、1986
AD　松井桂三
DE　松井桂三、清水栄治
CN　松井桂三、清水栄治
PH　村上ひろし
CL　ヒロココシノ
　　インターナショナル
手前の立体の穴から、向う側に印刷されたモデルの姿がのぞけるという遊び的要素をもった案内状

10
Invitation to Shop Opening, 1986
AD　Keizo Matsui
DE　Keizo Matsui
　　Eiji Shimizu
CN　Keizo Matsui
　　Eiji Shimizu
PH　Hiroshi Murakami
CL　Hiroko Koshino
　　International
The model printed on the other end of the flap can be seen from the hole of the cubic figure in front.
An invitation letter with playfulness

12
喜多俊之ニューヨーク個展案内状、1987
AD 松井桂三
DE 松井桂三
CL 喜多俊之
展示作品の一つ「二畳一間」が飛び出てくる。

12
Invitation to One-man Show of an Industrial Designer, 1987
AD Keizo Matsui
DE Keizo Matsui
CL Toshiyuki Kita
A sample of the exhibits jumps out.

11
トランク展示会案内状、1985
AD 松井桂三
DE 松井桂三、清水栄治
CL ヒロココシノ
   インターナショナル

11
Invitation to Exhibition, 1985
AD Keizo Matsui
DE Keizo Matsui
   Eiji Shimizu
CL Hiroko Koshino
   International

TOSHIYUKI KITA

"Internationally renowned industrial designer from Japan & Italy, applies traditional URUSHI lacquer techniques to common use objects creating works of elegance and spiritual substance for the 'Ceremony of everyday life.'"

October 6–November 23, 1991
Design Gallery 91
91 Grand Street
New York, NY 10013
Tuesday–Saturday 12 noon–6 pm

13

スポーツウェアカタログ, 1984
AD/DE デーヴィッド・エデルスタイン
　　　 ナンシー・エデルスタイン
　　　 ラニー・フレンチ
PH　　ジム・カミンス
　　　 ロッキー・サルスコフ
WR　　デーヴィッド・エデルスタイン
AG　　エデルスタイン・アソシエイツ(USA)
PR Co. ウィルキンズ＆ピーターソン
CL　　ジェネラ・スポーツウェア
ニューヨークADC金賞受賞

13

Catalogue, 1984
AD/DE David Edelstein
　　　 Nancy Edelstein
　　　 Lanny French
PH　　Jim Cummins
　　　 Rocky Salskov
WR　　David Edelstein
AG　　Edelstein Associates, Seattle, USA
PR Co. Wilkins & Peterson
CL　　Generra Sportswear
Art Directors Club New York
Gold Award Winner

14

募金依頼状、1987
DE　ジョイス・カルキン
CN　ジョイス・カルキン
AG　クラーク・ゴワード・フィッツ・デザイン(USA)
CL　ジョージ・マコンバー家

14

Fundraising for Building, 1987
DE　Joyce Culkin
CN　Joyce Culkin
AG　Clarke Goward Fitts Design, Boston, USA
CL　The George Macomber Family Residence

15
ダンロップ新製品案内状、1986
AD 三木 健
DE 三木 健
CN 三木 健
CL 日本ダンロップ
店頭での簡単なP.O.P.にも使用。

15
Announcement of
New Products, 1986
AD Ken Miki
DE Ken Miki
CN Ken Miki
CL Sumitomo Rubber
 Industries
This can be used as a P.O.P.
display tool.

16

16

名刺、1985
DE　ジョイス・カルキン
CN　ジョイス・カルキン
CL　ディメンショナル・デザイン
　　（USA）

16

Business Card, 1985
DE　Joyce Culkin
CN　Joyce Culkin
CL　Dimensional Design,
　　Massachusetts

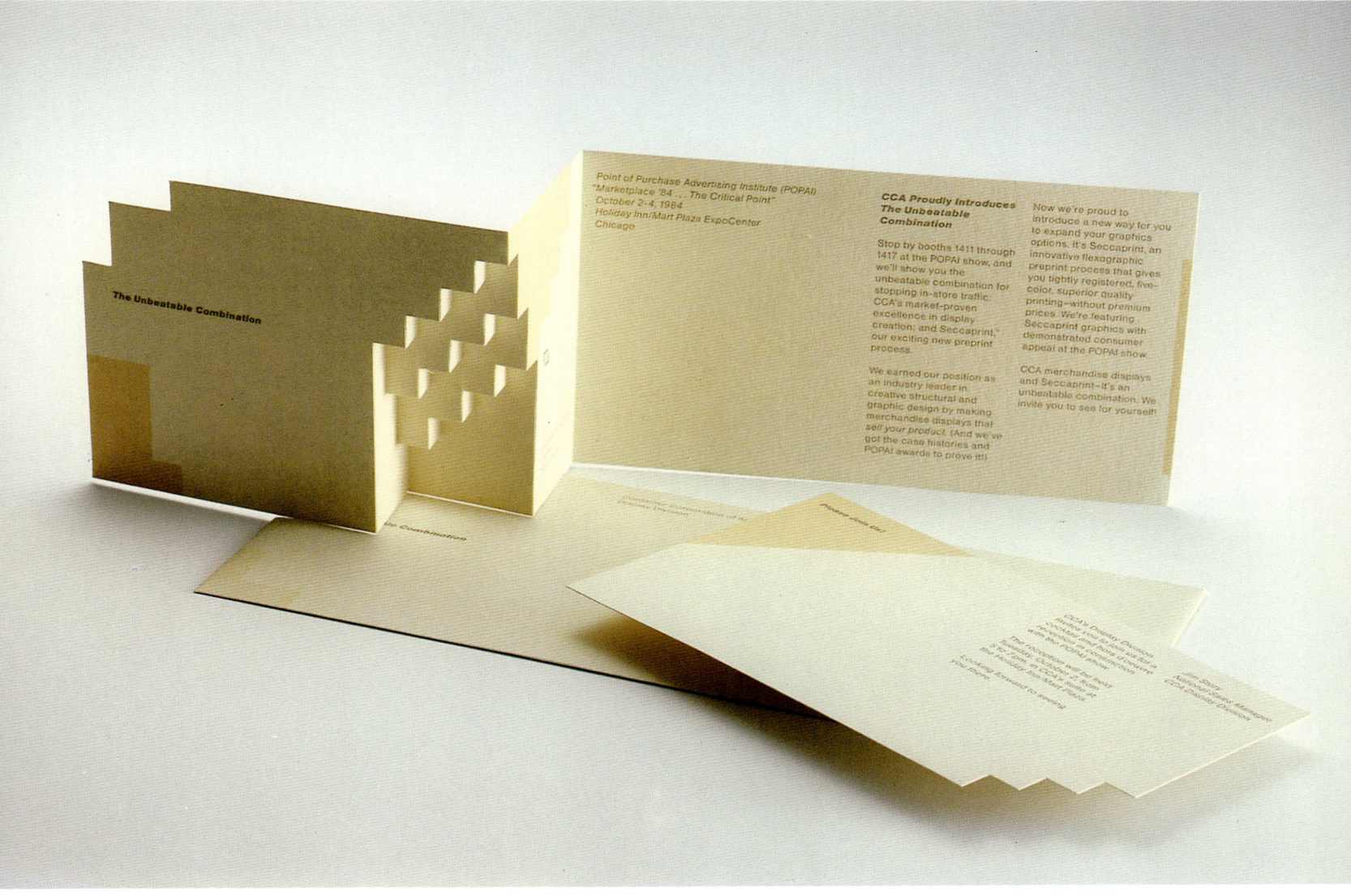

17
展示会案内・招待状、1985
DE ジョイス・カルキン
CN ジョイス・カルキン
CL コンテナ・コーポレーション・
   オブ・アメリカ (USA)

17
Announcement and Invitation
to Purchase Show, 1985
DE Joyce Culkin
CN Joyce Culkin
CL Container Corporation of
   America, Chicago

DIMENSIONAL
DESIGN

DIRECT MAIL
ANNOUNCEMENTS
INVITATIONS
POINT OF PURCHASE
CALENDARS
DISPLAY
PROMOTIONAL PACKAGING
SALES KITS
TABLE TENTS
MOBILES
PREMIUMS

JOYCE CULKIN   1514 BEACON ST.   BROOKLINE, MA 02146   617 • 731 • 9544

18

事務所案内状、1985
DE　ジョイス・カルキン
CN　ジョイス・カルキン
CL　ディメンショナル・デザイン
　　（USA）

18

Self-Promotion
Announcement, 1985
DE　Joyce Culkin
CN　Joyce Culkin
CL　Dimensional Design,
　　Massachusetts

19
名刺
DE/MA グラフィックス3

19
Business Card
DE/MA Graphics3

20

Direct Mail, 1984
AD M. Ray Gedeon
DE Philip Gell
PH Marty Stouffer
AG Conference Management, Ohio, USA
CL American Express Travel Related Services Company

Art Directors Club New York
Gold Award Winner

Zap!
We're all 20 years older and its time to celebrate. It's your 20 year class reunion and we've planned a great weekend. Friday, June 24, 1983 Garland high school girls gym 6 pm to 8 pm. Saturday, June 25, 1983 Lakewood Country Club, Dallas 7 pm to 12 pm. Dress for both gatherings is casual. After all . . . it's all for fun.

Here's your invitation to the event you've waited 20 years for...

1983

21

同窓会案内状、1984
AD　ケン・パフ
DE　ケン・パフ/パフ＆カンパニー (USA)
CL　ガーランド高等学校1963年クラス

1963年当時の写真と1963の数字が右のタブを引くと、現在の顔と1983の数字に変わる。ニューヨークADC銀賞受賞

21

Invitation to Class Reunion, 1984
AD　Ken Pugh
DE　Ken Pugh/Pugh & Company, Dallas, USA
CL　Garland High School Class of 1963

The photo of the class and the figure 1963 are replaced by the photo of 20 years later and the figure 1983 by pulling the tab. Art Directors Club New York Silver Award Winner

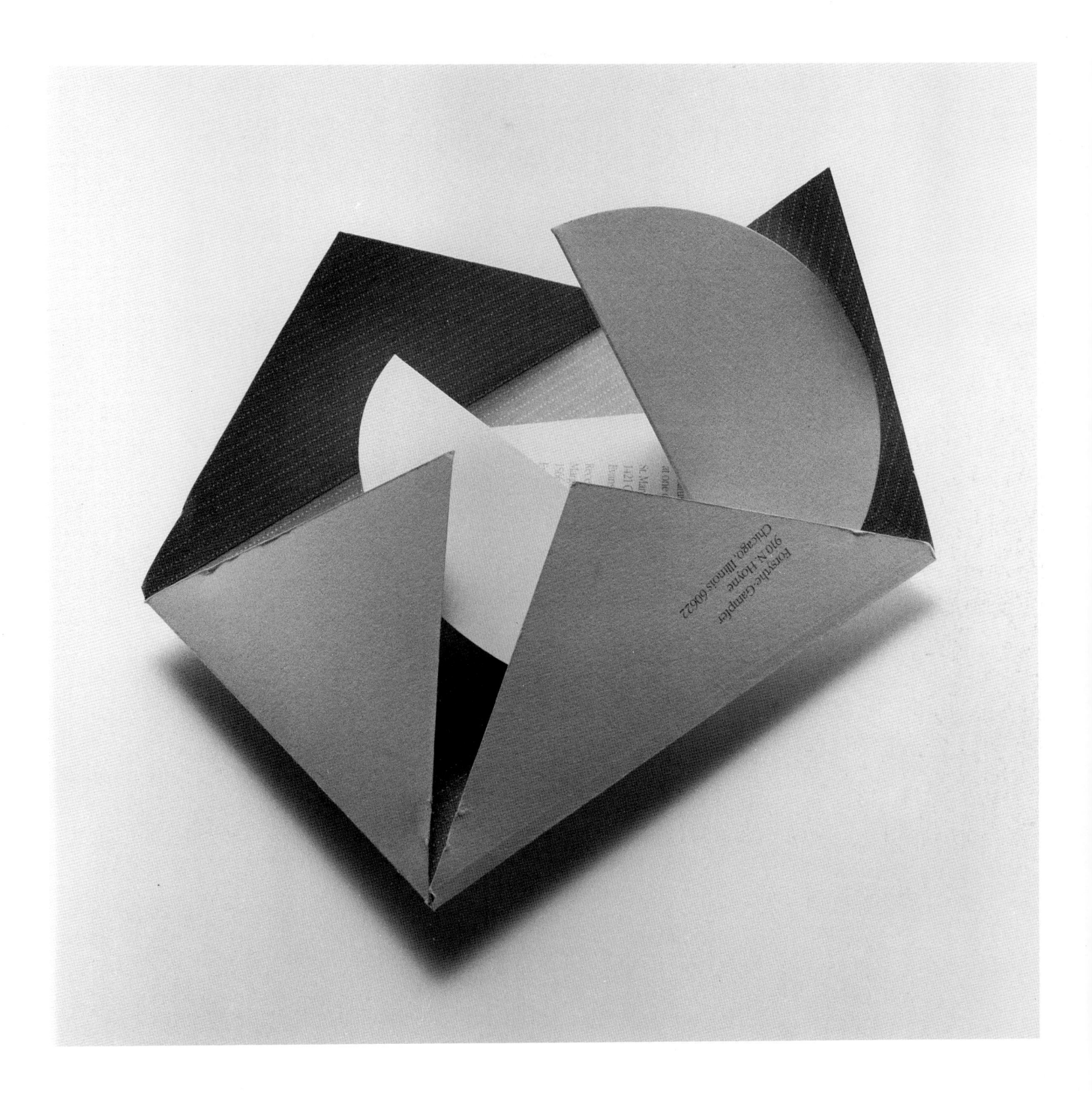

22
結婚式招待状、1984
DE　ジョイス・カルキン
CN　ジョイス・カルキン

22
Invitation to Wedding, 1984
DE　Joyce Cu kin
CN　Joyce Cuikin

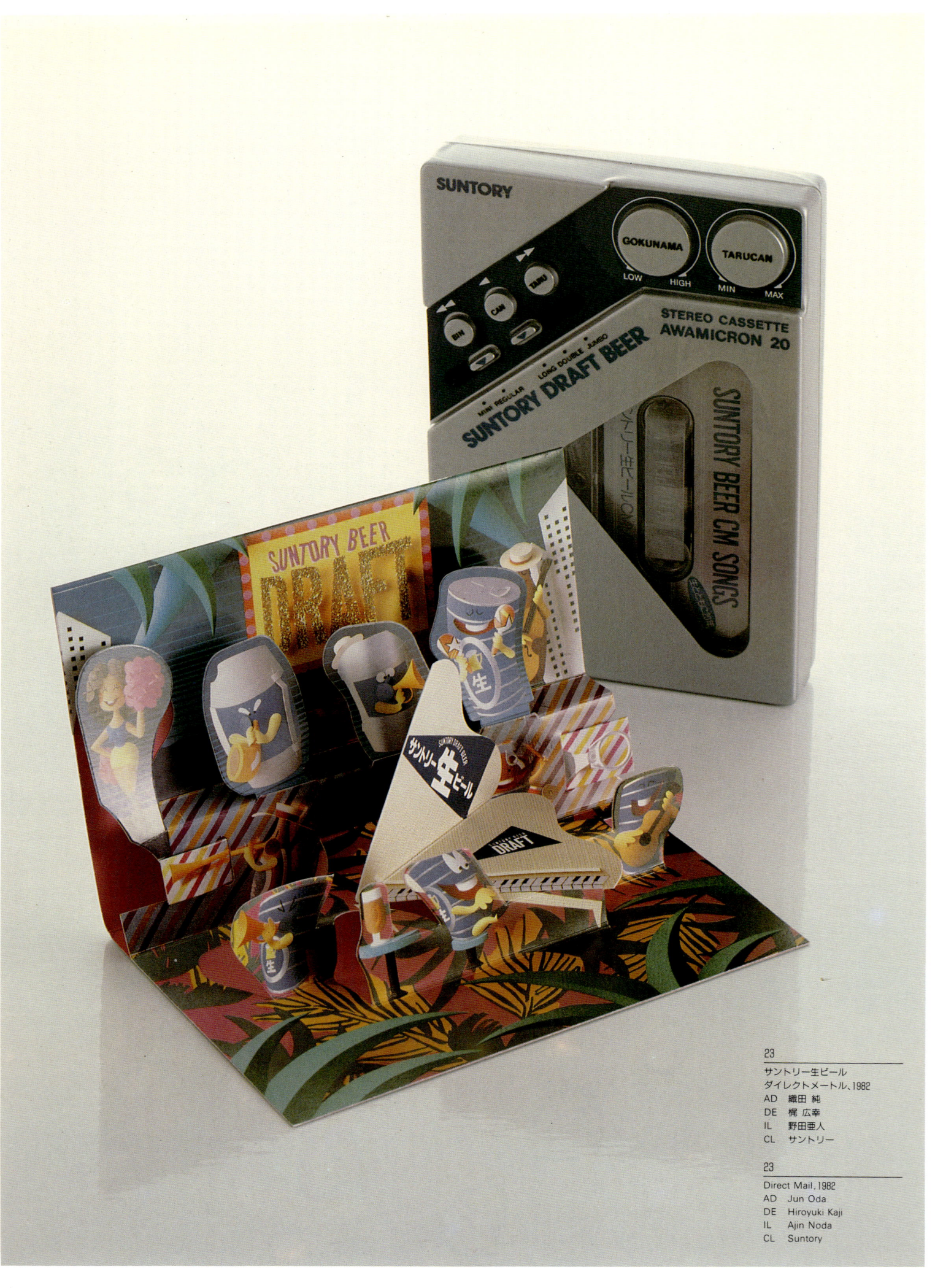

23
サントリー生ビール
ダイレクトメートル、1982
AD 織田 純
DE 梶 広幸
IL 野田亜人
CL サントリー

23
Direct Mail, 1982
AD Jun Oda
DE Hiroyuki Kaji
IL Ajin Noda
CL Suntory

24
アクションマックロード
ダイレクトメール、1984
AD 金岩秀和、高田 務
DE 島崎 淳、粥川久也
WR 赤井 宏
PH 千葉正夫
CL 松下電器産業

24
Direct Mail, 1984
AD Hidekazu Kanaiwa,
 Tsutomu Takada
DE Jun Shimazaki,
 Hisaya Kayukawa
WR Hiroshi Akai
PH Masao Chiba
CL Matsushita Electric
 Industrial

25
サントリー21ダイレクトメール、
1984
AD　久保田秀明
DE　泉谷賢三
IL　佐藤貞男
CL　サントリー

25
Direct Mail,1984
AD　Hideaki Kubota
DE　Kenzo Izutani
IL　Sadao Sato
CL　Suntory

43

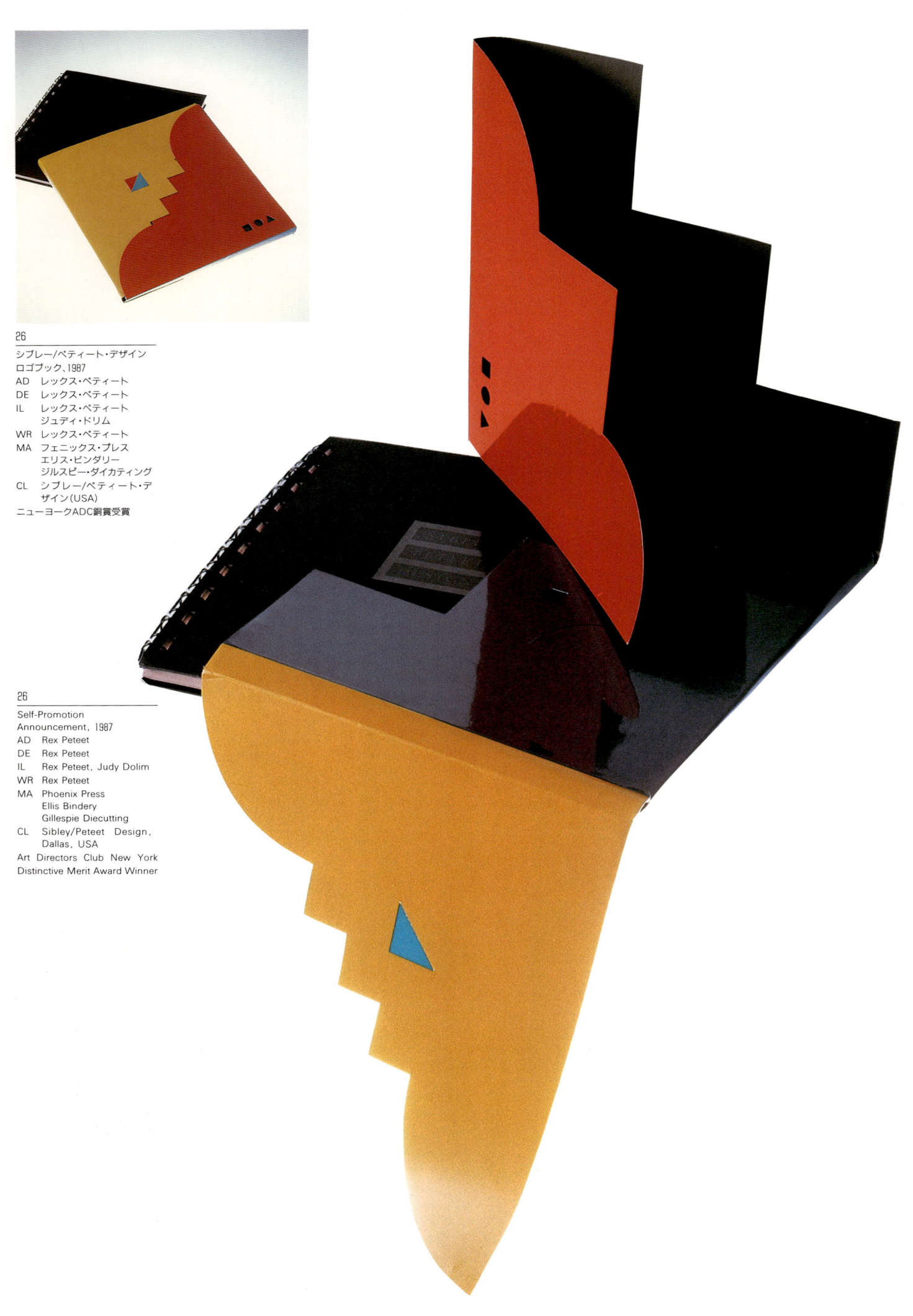

26
シブレー/ペティート・デザイン
ロゴブック、1987
AD　レックス・ペティート
DE　レックス・ペティート
IL　レックス・ペティート
　　ジュディ・ドリム
WR　レックス・ペティート
MA　フェニックス・プレス
　　エリス・ビンダリー
　　ジルスピー・ダイカティング
CL　シブレー/ペティート・デ
　　ザイン(USA)
ニューヨークADC銅賞受賞

26
Self-Promotion
Announcement, 1987
AD　Rex Peteet
DE　Rex Peteet
IL　Rex Peteet, Judy Dolim
WR　Rex Peteet
MA　Phoenix Press
　　Ellis Bindery
　　Gillespie Diecutting
CL　Sibley/Peteet Design,
　　Dallas, USA
Art Directors Club New York
Distinctive Merit Award Winner

27
ダイレクトメール、1984
AD　ウイリアム・ポーリン
DE　ドン・トラウズデル
PH　マイケル・グランベリー
WR　セイル・マッティングリー
AG　セリング・ソリューションズ
　　（USA）
CL　コカコーラ・USA
　　ディック・ダナ
ニューヨークADC銅賞受賞

27
Direct Mail, 1984
AD　William Paullin
DE　Don Trousdell
PH　Michael Granberry
WR　Ceil Mattingly
AG　Selling Solutions,
　　Atlanta, USA
CL　Coca-Cola USA
　　Dick Dana
Art Directors Club New York Distinctive Merit Award Winner

28
不老林ダイレクトメール、1985
AD 川崎修司
DE 川崎修司
WR 犬山達四郎
IL 安西水丸
MA 資生堂
CL 資生堂

28
Direct Mail, 1985
AD Shuji Kawasaki
DE Shuji Kawasaki
WR Tatsushiro Inuyama
IL Mizumaru Anzai
MA Shiseido
CL Shiseido

29

やまもと寛斎コレクション
春夏'85、1984
DE 高木 孝
IL 伊藤桂司
CL やまもと寛斎

29

Invitation to Fashion Show,
1984
DE Takashi Takagi
IL Keiji Ito
CL Kansai Yamamoto

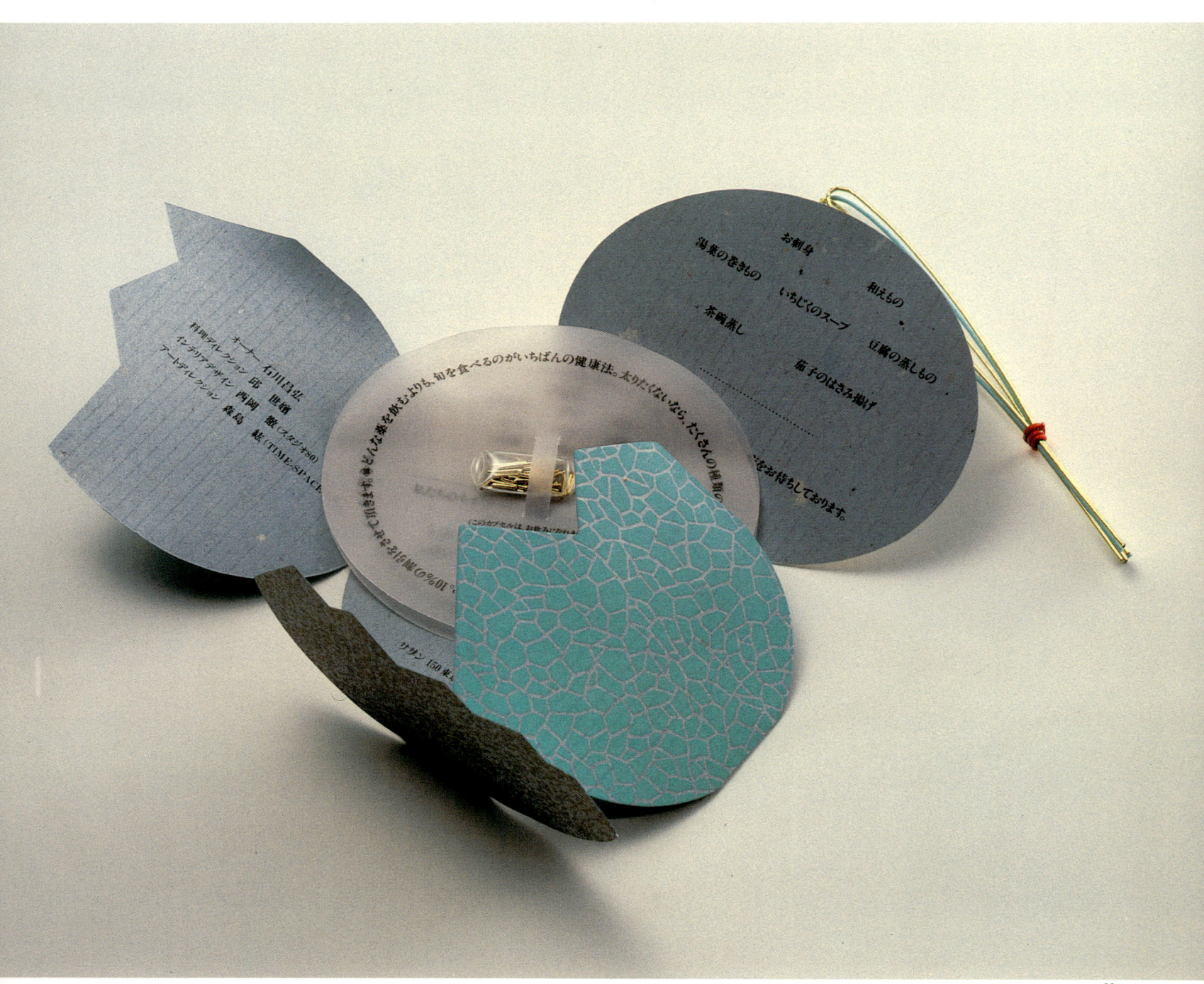

30a

30a・b

レストラン案内状、1986
AD 森島 紘
DE 森島 紘
WR 森島 紘
CL サザン

30a・b

Invitation to Chinese Restaurant, 1986
AD Hiroshi Morishima
DE Hiroshi Morishima
WR Hiroshi Morishima
CL Sasan

31a

31a・b

日本画展案内状、1985
AD 森島 紘
DE 森島 紘、駒形克巳
WR 河北倫明、梅原 猛
CL ワコール、京セラ
包みを開くと、節、空、巻、間、結、流、動、折、透、美を表現した10枚のカードが出てくる。ADC賞受賞

31a・b

Invitation to Japanese Painting Exhibition, 1985
AD Hiroshi Morishima
DE Hiroshi Morishima
   Katsumi Komagata
WR Michiaki Kawakita
   Takeshi Umehara
CL Wacoal, Kyocera
A set of ten cards each depicting a knot, vanity, a coil, an interval, a tie, a flow, movement, folding, transparency and beauty. ADC Award Winner

30b

TR - musubu.
To join strings
or ropes
together.
Also,
to become
branched or
reach maturity
and fruition.

BEAUTY – utsukushii
Beauty or appeal, and by extension which

EMPTINESS – ku
The sky, void, or the state of limbo. In Buddhism all things are regarded as being contained within "ku".

COIL – maku
To wind something into a roll or a coil — also used to describe the vortices and eddies formed in waves.

NODE – fushi
A node on a bamboo or a reed, and by extension a description of the turning points in one's life.

32a
32b

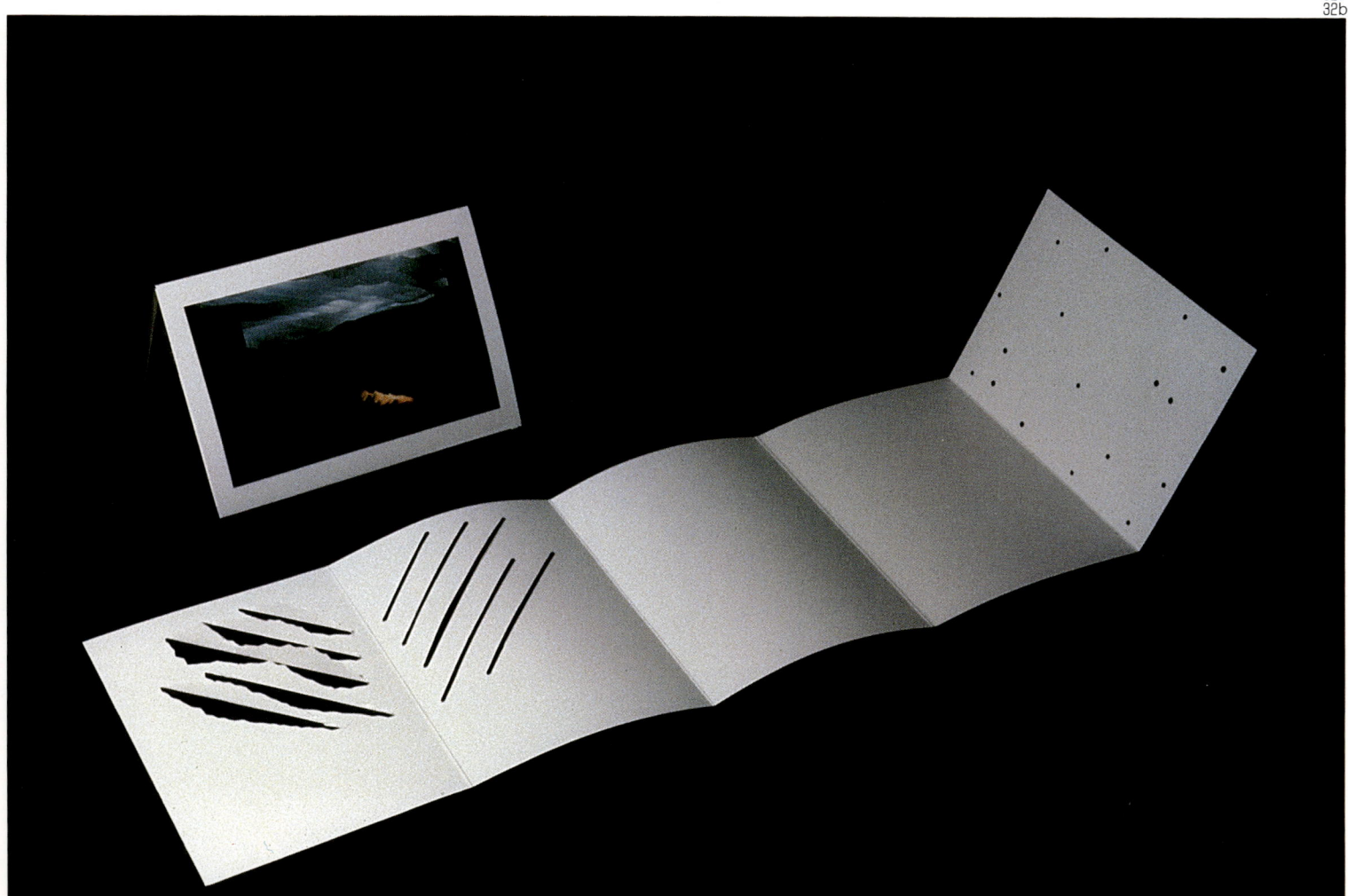

52

32a・b
レジデンス・オ・ラック
グリーティングカード、1984
AD　エミリオ・アンバース
DE　エミリオ・アンバース
MA　ルガーノ・グラフィカ
　　（スイス）
CL　インモビリアレ・カヴェル
　　ツァシオ

32a・b
Residence au lac
Greeting Card, 1984
AD　Emilio Ambasz
DE　Emilio Ambasz
MA　Lugano Grafica,
　　Switzerland
CL　Immobiliare Caverzasio

33a

33b

33a・b
ブリュッセル・ランベール銀行
グリーティングカード、1984
AD　エミリオ・アンバース
DE　エミリオ・アンバース
MA　グラフィス（イタリア）
CL　ブリュッセル・ランベール
　　銀行、ニューヨーク
ニューヨーク支店の1周年を記念
したカード

33a・b
Banque Bruxelles Lambert
Greeting Card, 1984
AD　Emilio Ambasz
DE　Emilio Ambasz
MA　Grafis, Italy
CL　Banque Bruxelles
　　Lambert, New York
Memorial card of one-year anniversary of opening New York branch bank

WATTS DISTRICT

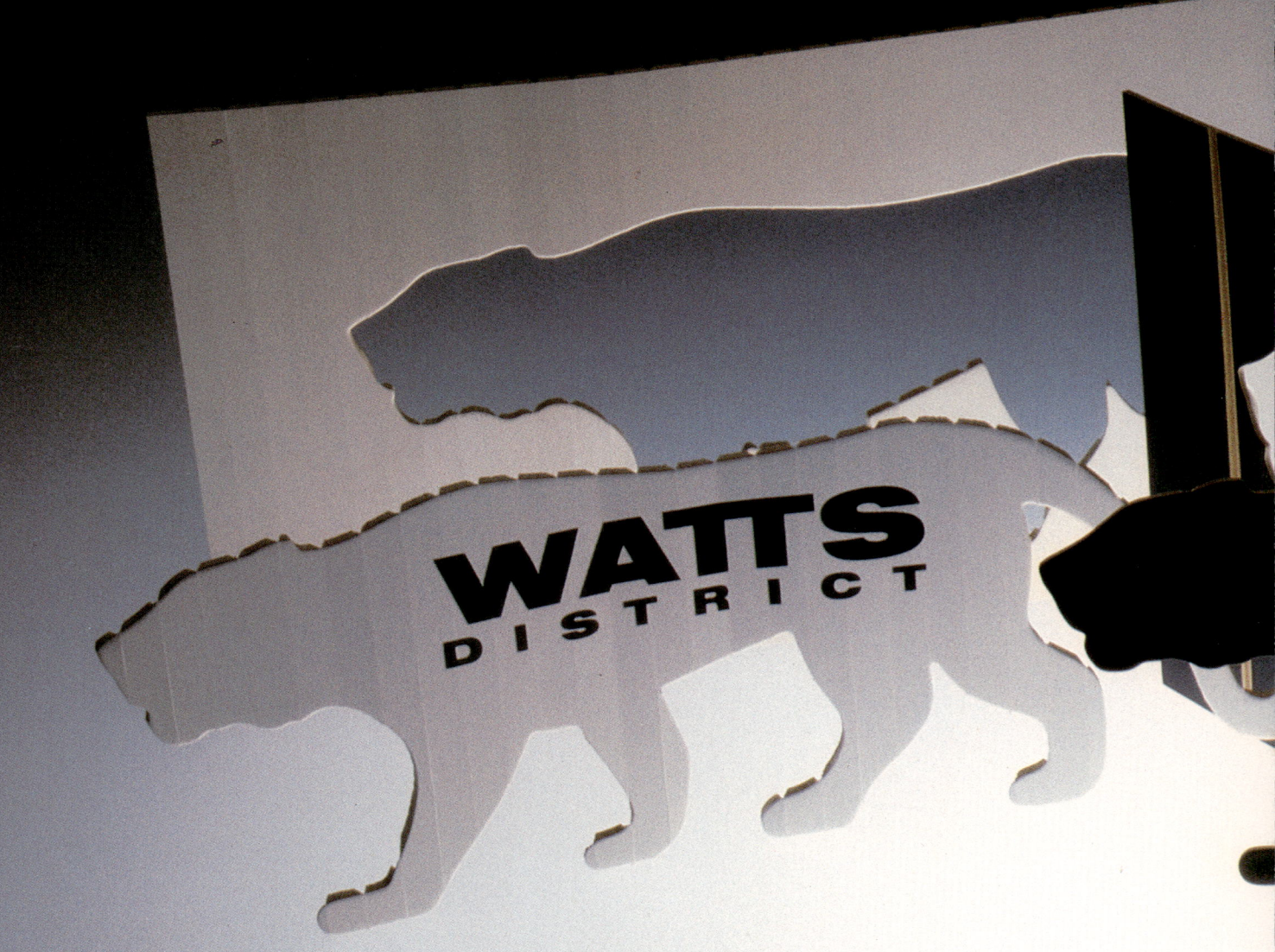

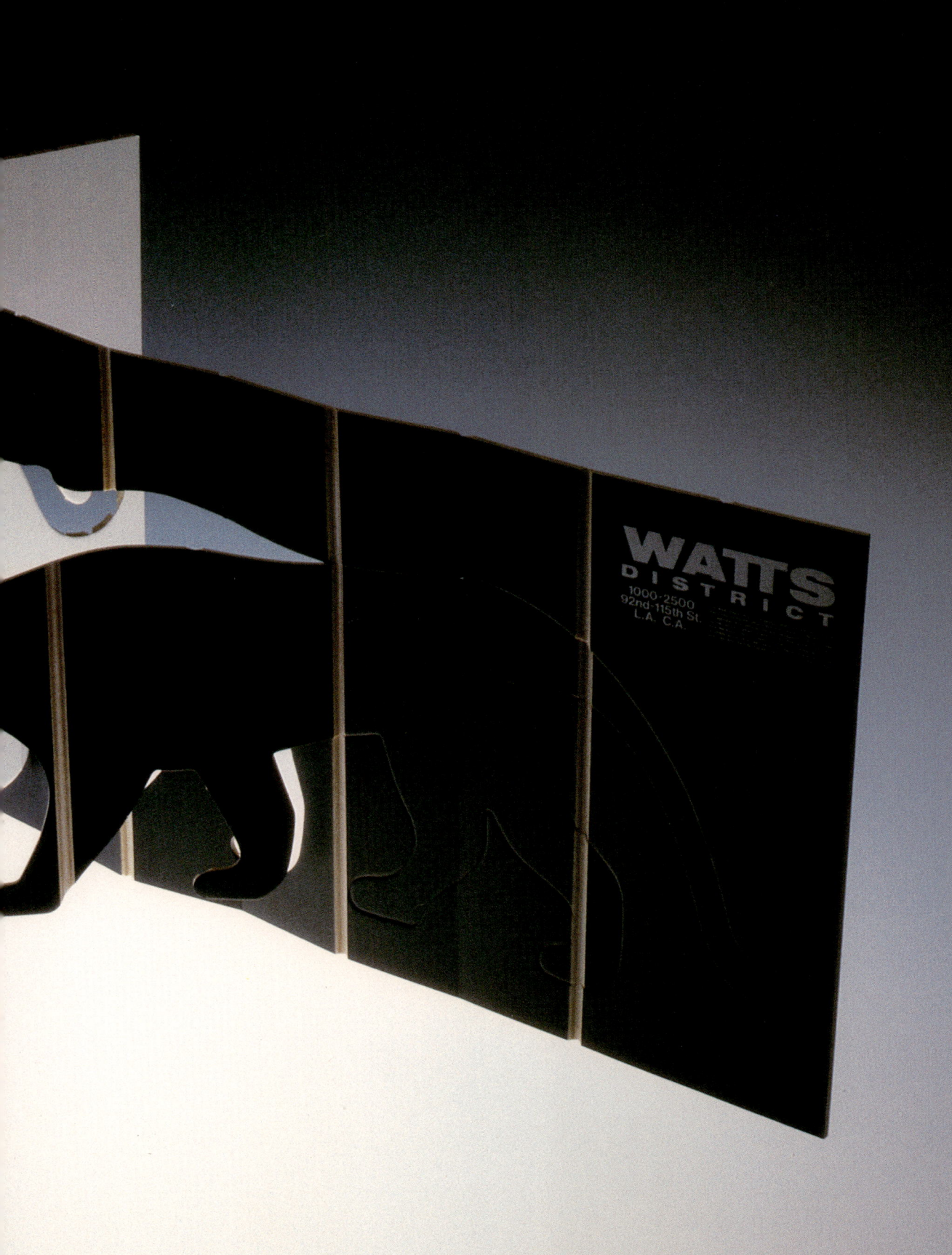

34
クネクネアニマル、1987
DE 柿本博康
MA 明星工芸
CL ライブハウス
　　ワッツディスクリクト

34
Wooden Card, 1987
DE Hiroyasu Kakimoto
MA Myojo Woodpack
CL Live House
　　Watts Discrict

35

佐藤貞夫展
EXCITING
DA DA DA DA
5月1日 2日
AM11:00~PM7:00
PM6:00より
オープニングパーティを開きます。
Sadao

Sadao

36

35
ダイナマイト、1984
DE 奥村昭夫
    パッケージングクリエイト
CL 佐藤貞夫

35
Invitation to Exhibition, 1984
DE Akio Okumura
    Packaging Create
CL Sacao Sato

36
ショールーム案内状、1983
DE 松本高明
AG エムプラスエム(USA)
CL ノルインターナショナル
    (USA)
中央の四角く切り取られた部分が、新しいショールームの場所を示している。

36
Invitation to Show Room, 1983
DE Takaaki Matsumoto
AG M Plus M, New York
CL Knoll International, New York
The cut in the center shows the location of the new showroom.

37

プレビュー、1987
AD　三木 健
DE　三木 健
MA　三木 健
CL　小谷和裁所
大阪ミナミにオープンしたヴィヴィッドライフビルプレビューの招待状。ほんの少しの風で糸でつながれた人物が遊泳する。

37

Invitation Card, 1987
AD　Ken Miki
DE　Ken Miki
MA　Ken Miki
CL　Jastec Kotani
An invitation letter of Vivid Life Building in downtown Osaka. With a breath of air, figures tied with strings swim in air.

38a·b

パーティ招待状、1985
AD　リン・フラーヒン
DE　ケビン・ペリー
MA　ピーター・ハル & アソシエイツ/ペーパー・パワー
CL　ペーパーパワー
封筒から出すと、ジャンプして招待状が飛び出てくる。

38a·b

Invitation to Party, 1985
AD　Lyn Hourahine
DE　Kevin Perry
MA　Peter Hull & Associates/ Paper Power
CL　Paper Power
An invitation letter jumps up when the envelope is opened.

39a
39b

39a・b
ロバート・ベントゥーリ
家具コレクション案内状、1984
AD ハロルド・マトッシアン
　　松本高明
DE 松本高明
AG ノルグラフィックス
CL ノルインターナショナル
　　（USA）
ポスターが折り込まれて入っている案内状

39a・b
Invitation to Robert Venturi
Furniture Collection, 1984
AD Harold Matossian,
　　Takaaki Matsumoto
DE Takaaki Matsumoto
AG Knoll Graphics
CL Knoll International,
　　New York
An invitation letter with a poster folded attached

40
―――――
移転案内状、1987
DE 松本高明
AG エムプラスエム (USA)
CL 松本高明
タブを下げると、タブに印刷され
た住所が現われる。

40
―――――
Office-Moving Announcement,
1987
DE Takaaki Matsumoto
AG M Plus M, New York
CL Takaaki Matsumoto
When the tab is turned, the
new address shows itself.

A TAG ISN'T ALWAYS THE TICKET.

41
ダイレクトメール、1985
AD　アン・ジョーンズ
DE　アン・ジョーンズ
WR　ジム・マーフィ
IL　アン・ジョーンズ
CL　ポピュラーフォトグラフィ

41
Direct Mail, 1985
AD　Anne Jones
DE　Anne Jones
WR　Jim Murphy
IL　Anne Jones
CL　Popular Photography

42
ダイレクトメール、1987
AD　アン・ジョーンズ
DE　アン・ジョーンズ
WR　アン・ジョーンズ
　　　アラン・デクスハイマー
IL　ランディ・スクース
CL　ポピュラーフォトグラフィ
カメラの部分が別紙になっている。

42
Direct Mail, 1987
AD　Anne Jones
DE　Anne Jones
WR　Anne Jones
　　　Alan Dexheimer
IL　Randy Scouth
CL　Popular Photography
The "camera" is made separately.

43a・b	**44**
おとなの色メガネメルヘン、1986	千秋楽きもの市、1986
CD 横井紘一	CD 吉田正歳
AD 木村正彦	AD 小林啓巳
DE 木村正彦	DE 小林啓巳
WR 松形規子	WR 西田茂数
IL 木村正彦、野木まゆみ、永田麻美	IL 梶栗健児
MA タッド	MA タッド
CL ファッションプラザ	CL 大阪高島屋

43a・b	**44**
Direct Mail, 1986	Direct Mail, 1986
CD Koichi Yokoi	CD Masatoshi Yoshida
AD Masahiko Kimura	AD Hiromi Kobayashi
DE Masahiko Kimura	DE Hiromi Kobayashi
WR Noriko Matsukata	WR Shigekazu Nishida
IL Masahiko Kimura, Mayumi Nogi, Asami Nagata	IL Kenji Kajikuri
MA Tad	MA Tad
CL Fashion Plaza	CL Osaka Takashimaya

東
「本日の好取組」
感謝大奉仕!
三〇年に一度の
西
「本日の好取組」
千秋楽 きもの市
これより十両
一〇万円均一
髙島屋
千秋楽
結びの一番
特別出品
超豪華逸品呉服 特別奉仕
和装小物 特別奉仕
出場部屋
風流相撲茶屋特設
昭和六十一年十一月二十五日
不許複製

45

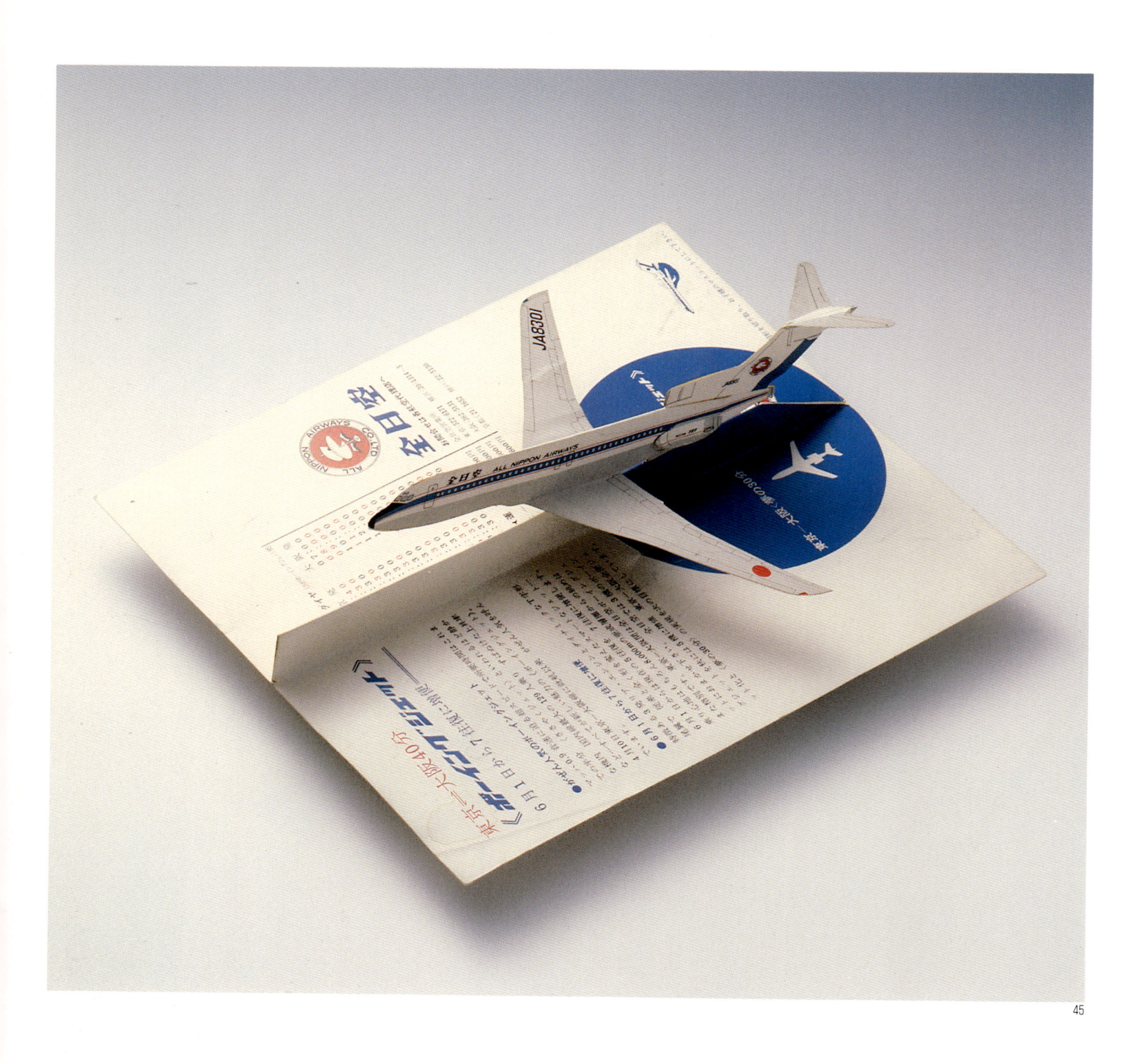

45	45	46a・b	46a・b	47	47
全日空リーフレット、1964	Leaflet, 1964	ソニーカラーテレビパンフレット、1963	Pamphlet, 1963	ソニービル落成記念パンフレット、1966	Pamphlet, 1966
DE 宮川昭二	DE Shoji Miyagawa	DE 宮川昭二	DE Shoji Miyagawa	AD 黒木靖夫	AD Yasuo Kuroki
MA 図書印刷	MA Tosho Printing	CN 宮川昭二	CN Shoji Miyagawa	CN 宮川昭二	CN Shoji Miyagawa
CL 全日空	CL All Nippon Airways	CL ソニー	CL Sony	CL ソニー	CL Sony
全日空が初めてジェット機を導入したのを記念して制作された。	A leaflet produced to commemorate ANA's introduction of jet-liners	タブを引くと白黒がカラーに変わる。テレビの初のカラー化導入を視覚的に示唆。	When the tab is pulled, the color changes. A visual indication of introduction of color-TV	ビルの竣工を記念して制作された。	This pamphlet was created to mark the completion of SONY Building.

46a

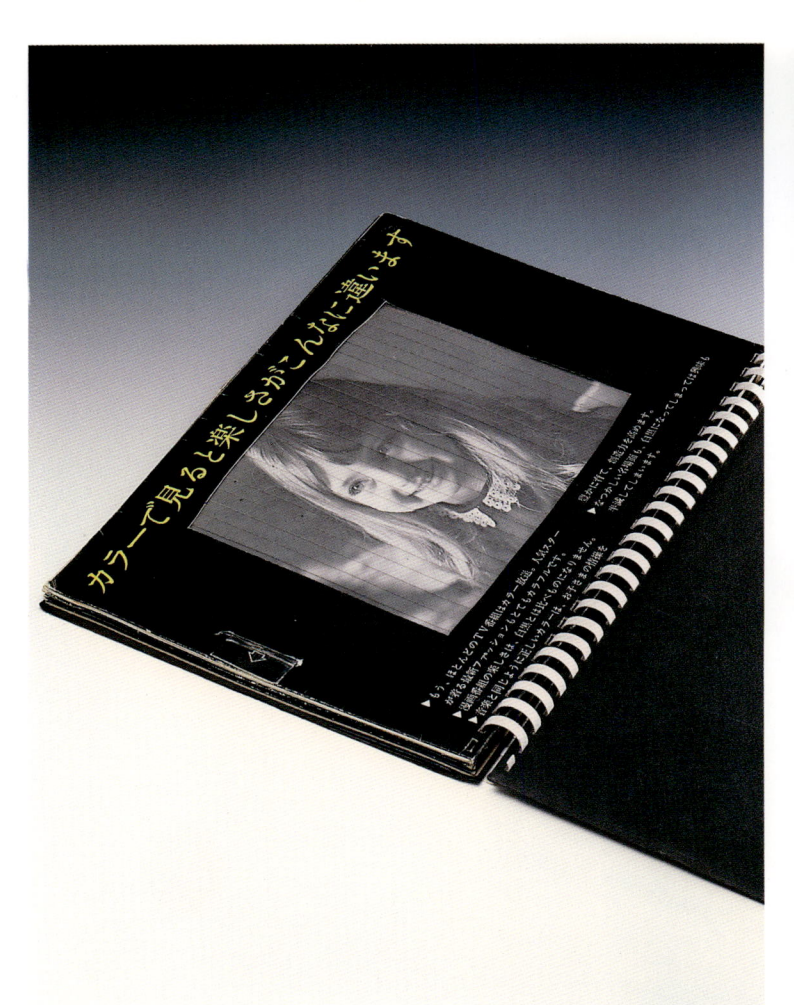

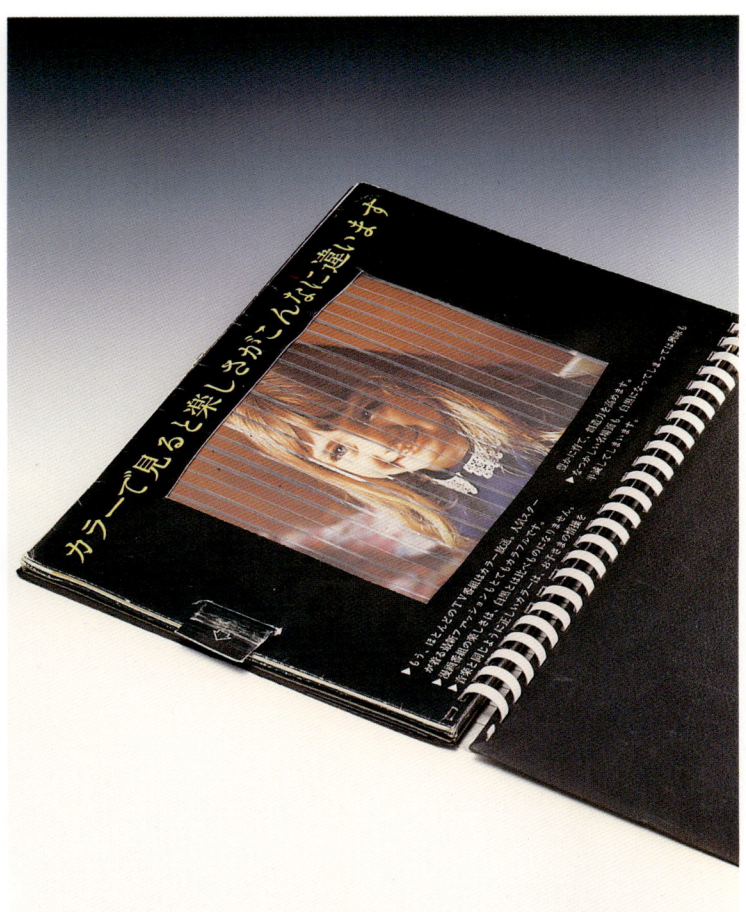

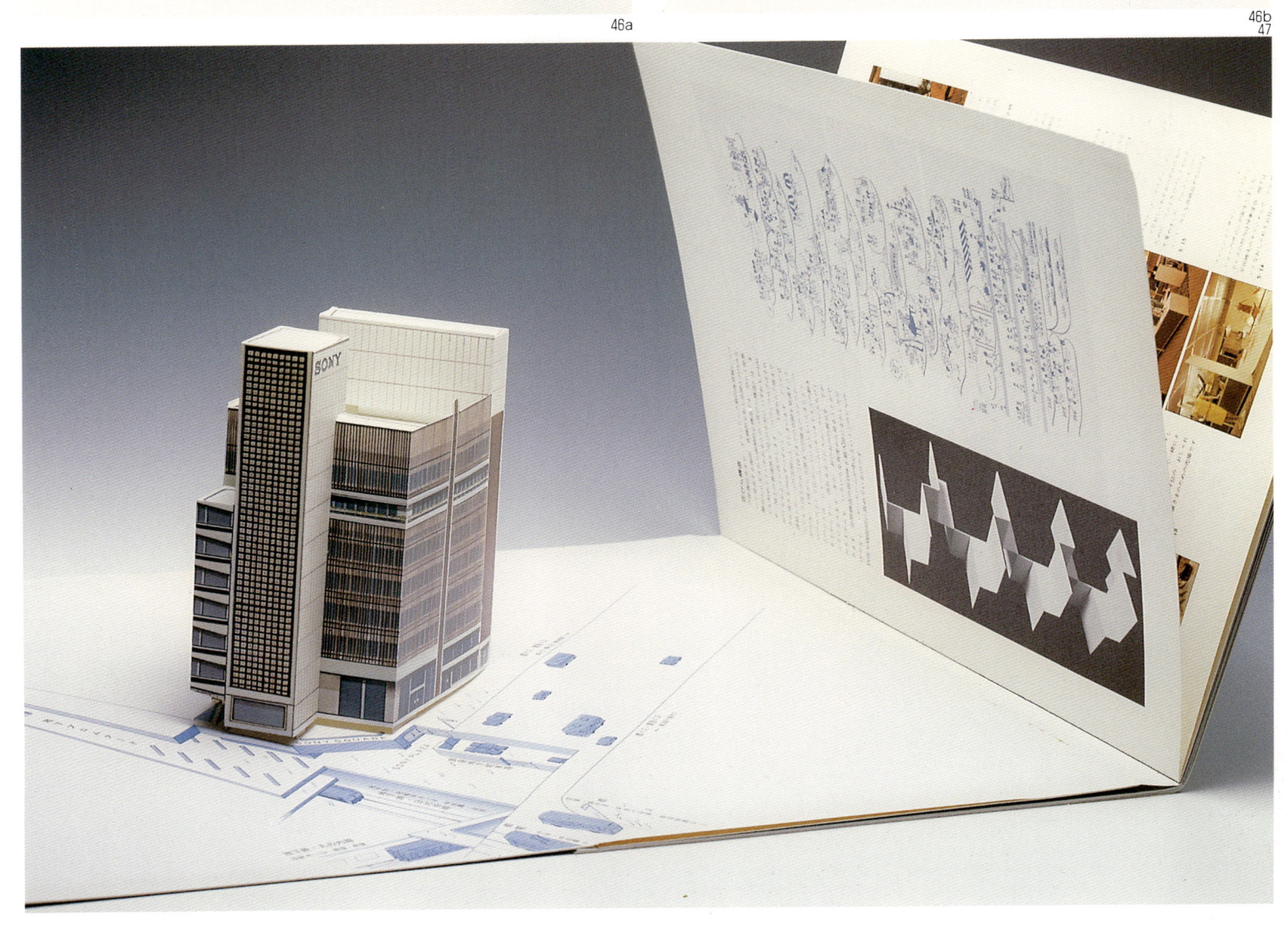

46b

67

CHRISTMAS AND NEW YEAR'S CARDS
BIRTHDAY CARDS
OTHER GREETING CARDS
・
クリスマスカード
年賀状
バースデーカード
グリーティングカード

ポップアップ
グリーティングカード、1985
AD　ロッド・シュラガー
DE　リン・フラーヒン
　　　ケビン・ペリー
CN　リン・フラーヒン
IL　キャシー・ワイアット
　　　ピーター・ビーヴィス
CL　セカンド・ネーチャー

Pop-Up Greeting Card, 1985
AD　Rod Shrager
DE　Lyn Hourahine, Kevin Perry
CN　Lyn Hourahine
IL　Kathy Wyatt, Peter Beavis
CL　Second Nature

48

49

50

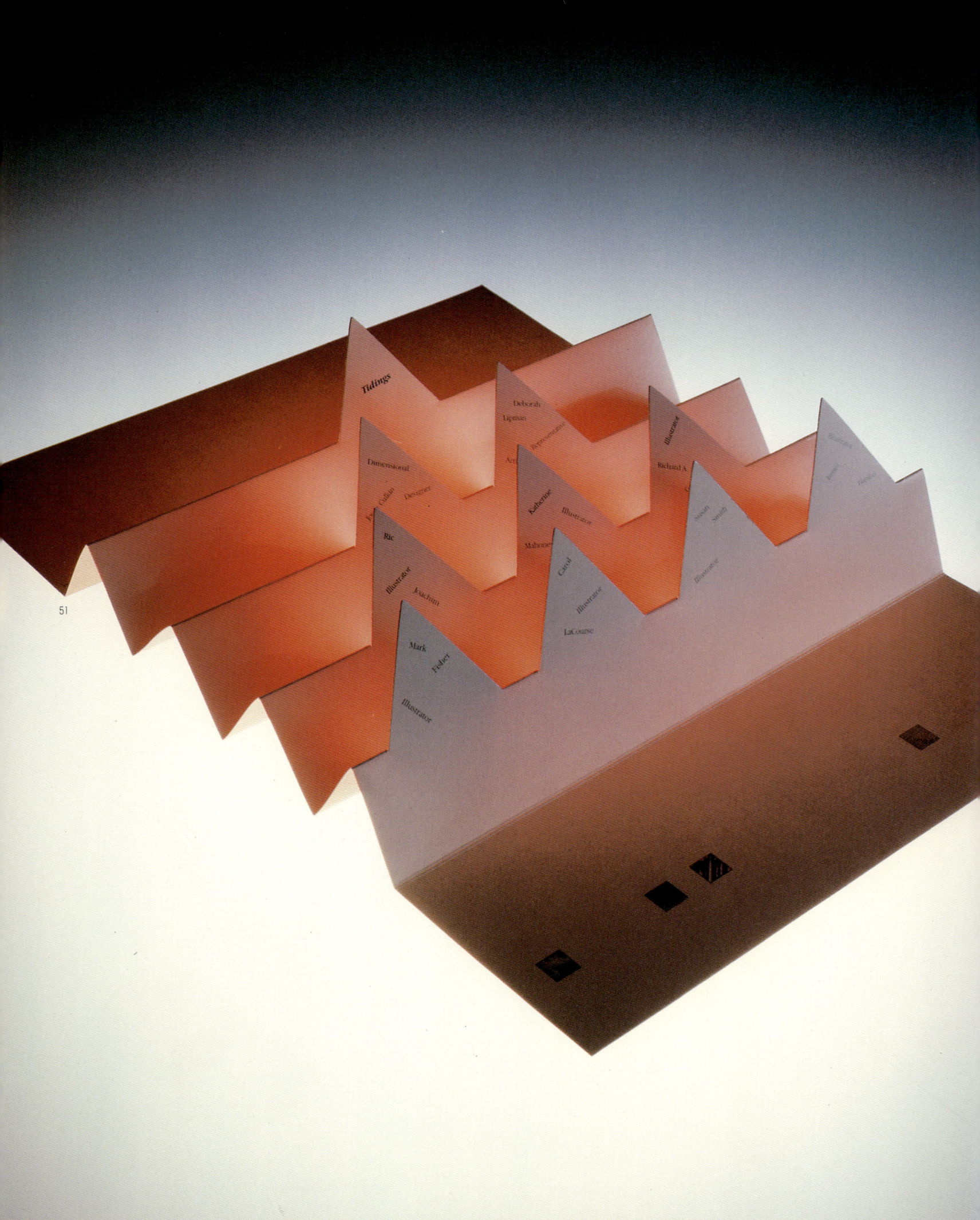

51

48
スノーフレーク、1983
AD　リン・フラーヒン
MA　ピーター・ハル&アソシエ
　　イツ/ペーパー・パワー
CL　リン・フラーヒン・デザイン
　　アソシエイツ

48
Christmas Card 'Snowflake',
1983
AD　Lyn Hourahine
MA　Peter Hull & Associates/
　　Paper Power
CL　Lyn Hourahine Design
　　Associates

49
段状のクリスマスツリー、1986
AD　リン・フラーヒン
DE　リン・フラーヒン
MA　ピーター・ハル&アソシエ
　　イツ/ペーパー・パワー
CL　リン・フラーヒン・デザイン
　　アソシエイツ&ペーパー・パワー

49
Christmas Card
'Stepped Christmas Tree', 1986
AD　Lyn Hourahine
DE　Lyn Hourahine
MA　Peter Hull & Associates /
　　Paper Power
CL　Lyn Hourahine Design
　　Associates & Paper Power

50
クリスマスツリー、1984
AD　リン・フラーヒン
DE　リン・フラーヒン
MA　ピーター・ハル & アソシエ
　　イツ/ペーパー・パワー
CL　リン・フラーヒン・デザイン
　　アソシエイツ

50
Christmas Tree Card, 1984
AD　Lyn Hourahine
DE　Lyn Hourahine
MA　Peter Hull & Associates/
　　Paper Power
CL　Lyn Hourahine Design
　　Associates

51
クリスマスカード、1986
DE　ジョイス・カルキン
CN　ジョイス・カルキン
CL　デボラ・リドマウ・アーティ
　　スツ・リプレゼンタティブ
　　(USA)

51
Christmas Card, 1986
DE　Joyce Culkin
CN　Joyce Culkin
CL　Deborah Lidmaw Artist's
　　Representative, Boston,
　　USA

52
グリーティングカード
DE　ペイン・ファミリー・カード
　　(イギリス)

52
Greeting Card
DE　Payne Family Cards,
　　England

73

merry christmas

© 1985. Paper Power

53a

53b

53a・b

星、1985

AD　リン・フラーヒン
DE　ケビン・ペリー
MA　ピーター・ハル&アソシエイツ/ペーパー・パワー
CL　リン・フラーヒン・デザイン　アソシエイツ&ペーパー・パワー

53a・b

Christmas Card 'Star', 1985

AD　Lyn Hourahine
DE　Kevin Perry
MA　Peter Hull & Associates/ Paper Power
CL　Lyn Hourahine Design Associates & Paper Power

54

54
年賀状、1980
DE/CL 奥村昭夫
パッケージングクリエイト

54
New Year's Card, 1980
DE/CL Akio Okumura
Packaging Create

55a・b
年賀状、1983
DE/CL 奥村昭夫
パッケージングクリエイト

55a・b
New Year's Card, 1983
DE/CL Akio Okumura
Packaging Create

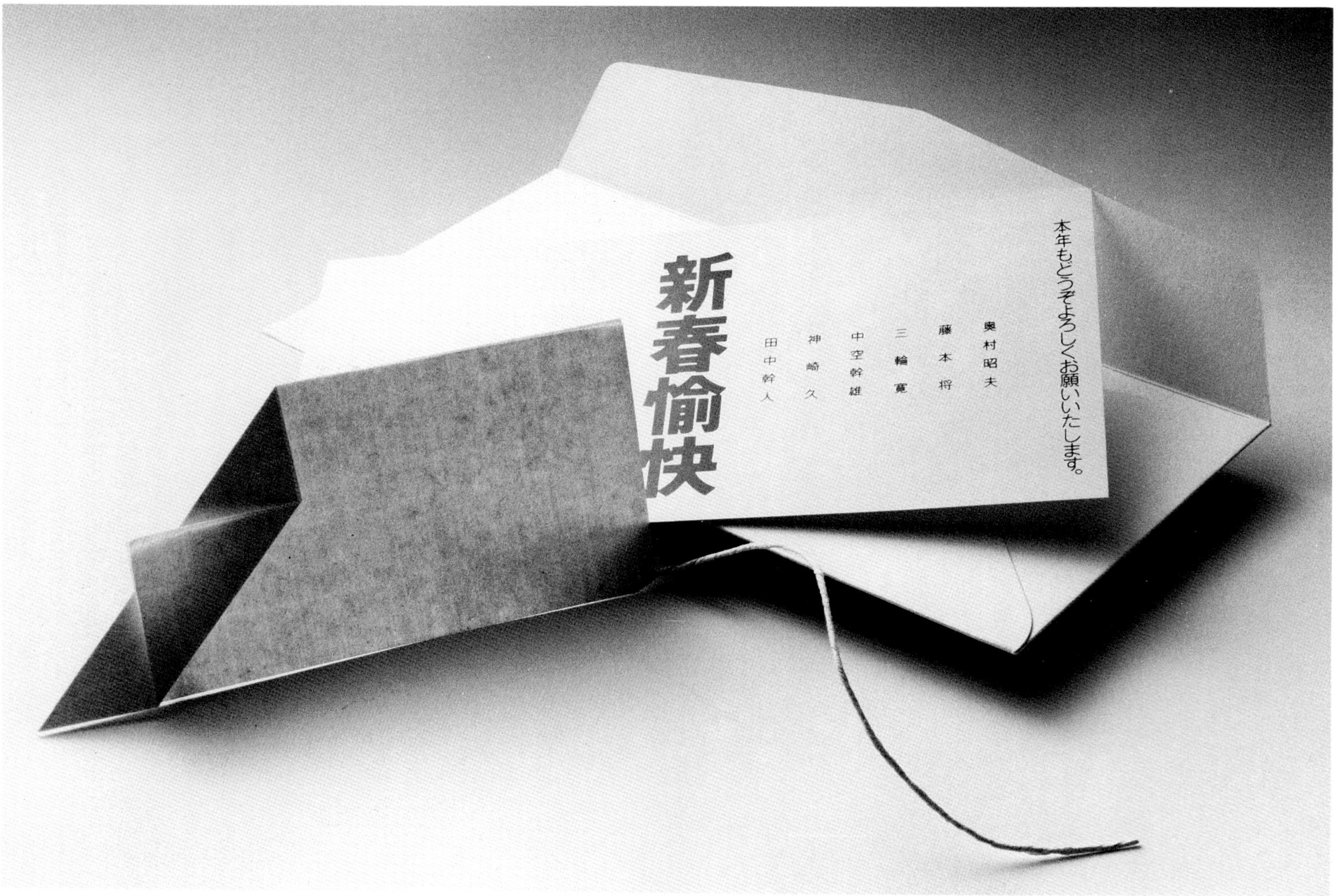
新春愉快
本年もどうぞよろしくお願いいたします。
奥村昭夫
藤本将
三輪寛
中空幹雄
神崎久
田中幹人

56
57

新春
本年もどうぞよろしくお願いいたしま
奥村昭夫
藤本将
神崎久
田中幹人
本多厚士

56
年賀状、1984
DE/CL 奥村昭夫
　　　　パッケージングクリエイト

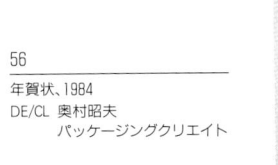

56
New Year's Card, 1984
DE/CL Akio Okumura
　　　　Packaging Create

57
年賀状、1985
DE/CL 奥村昭夫
　　　　パッケージングクリエイト

57
New Year's Card, 1985
DE/CL Akio Okumura
　　　　Packaging Create

58a・b
年賀状、1976
DE/CL 奥村昭夫
　　　　パッケージングクリエイト

58a・b
New Year's Card, 1976
DE/CL Akio Okumura
　　　　Packaging Create

59
―――――――
年賀状、1977
DE/CL 奥村昭夫
　　　パッケージングクリエイト

59
―――――――
New Year's Card, 1977
DE/CL Akio Okumura
　　　Packaging Create

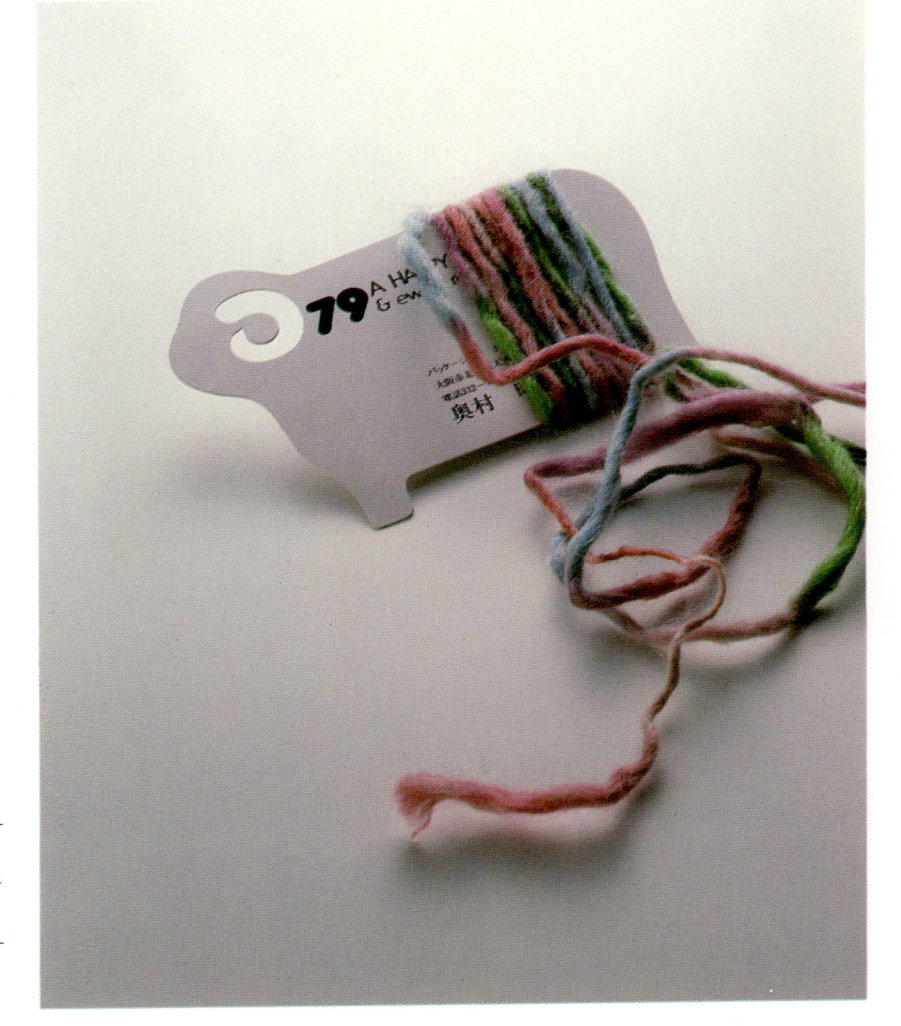

60a・b

年賀状、1979
DE/CL 奥村昭夫
パッケージングクリエイト

60a・b

New Year's Card, 1979
DE/CL Akio Okumura
Packaging Create

61

61・62
グリーティングカード、1982
DE 茶谷正洋
CN 茶谷正洋

61・62
Greeting Card, 1982
DE Masahiro Chatani
CN Masahiro Chatani

63a・b

サンタBOX、1985
DE　田代耕司
CL　ペイラム
箱の正面の両端を交互に押すと、動物とサンタクロースの顔が出たり入ったりする。

63a・b

Christmas Card, 1985
DE　Koji Tashiro
CL　Peiram
When the edges of the front face are pushed alternately, an animal and Santa Claus comes up and down.

64
グリーティングカード
DE　R.E.ジョーダン
CL　ホールマーク

64
Greeting Card
DE　R.E.Jordan
CL　Hallmark

65
PEACE、1984
DE 田代耕司
MA 田代耕司

65
Christmas Card, 1984
DE Koji Tashiro
MA Koji Tashiro

66
Dear Tomoko、1984
AD 三木 健
DE 三木 健
MA 三木 健

66
Greeting Card, 1984
AD Ken Miki
DE Ken Miki
MA Ken Miki

67

あやとり、1981
AD 三木 健
DE 三木 健
MA 三木 健
CL フジエテキスタイル

67

Greeting Card, 1981
AD Ken Miki
DE Ken Miki
MA Ken Miki
CL Fujie Textile

68

68

Thank you, 1981
AD　三木 健
DE　三木 健
MA　三木 健
CL　三木健デザイン事務所

68

Greeting Card, 1981
AD　Ken Miki
DE　Ken Miki
MA　Ken Miki
CL　Ken Miki Design Office

69

流れ星、1981
AD 三木 健
DE 三木 健
MA 三木 健
CL 世界文化社
たてると、星がくるくると流れていくカード

69

Greeting Card, 1981
AD Ken Miki
DE Ken Miki
MA Ken Miki
CL Sekai Bunka-sha
Stars go round as the card is stood.

70

らくだ、1981
AD 三木 健
DE 三木 健
MA 三木 健
CL 三木健デザイン事務所

70

Late Summer Greeting Card,
1981
AD Ken Miki
DE Ken Miki
MA Ken Miki
CL Ken Miki Design Office

71

退院通知、1981
DE 三木 健
MA 三木 健

71

Announcement of Leaving the
Hospital, 1981
DE Ken Miki
MA Ken Miki

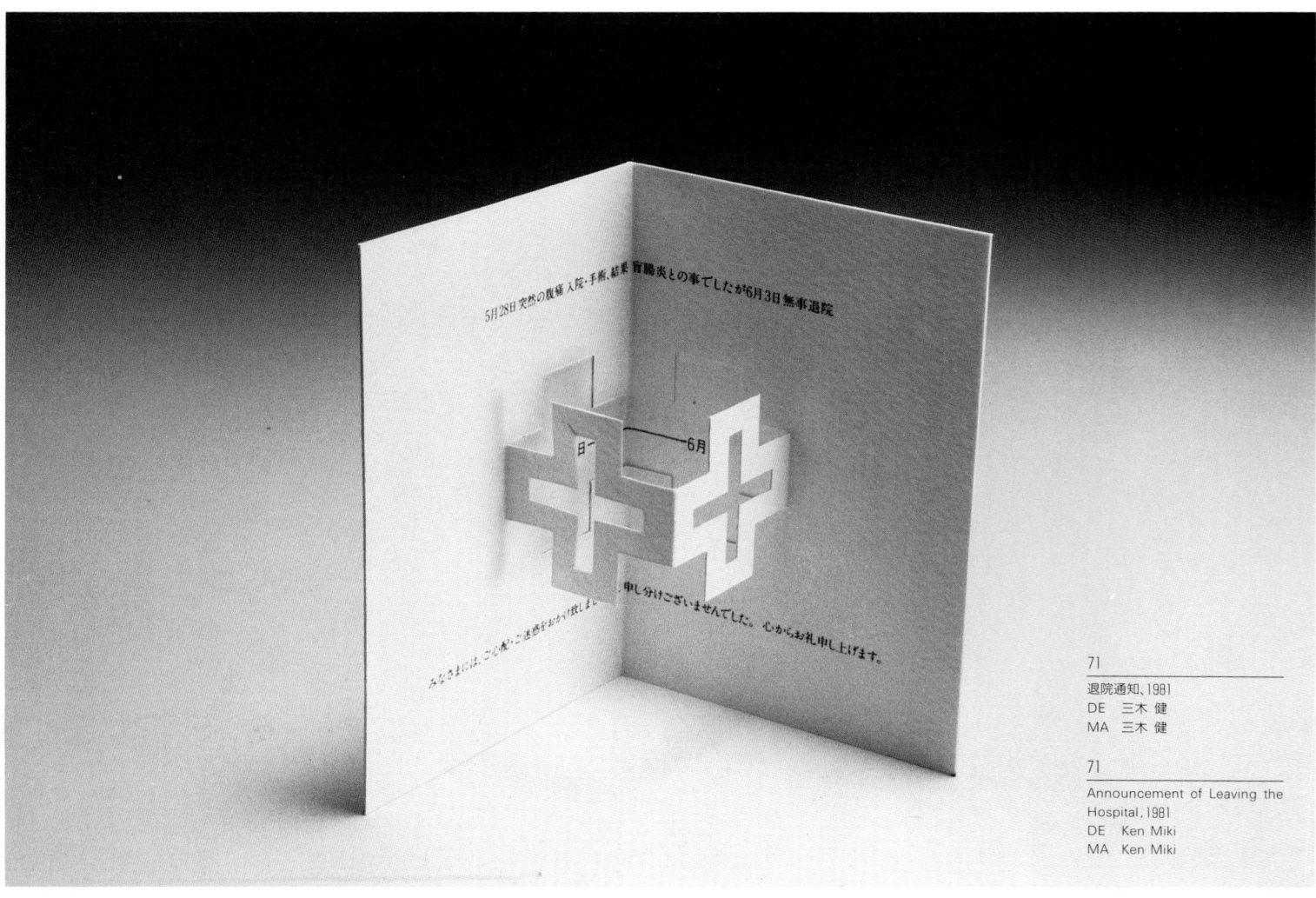

72
Midnight Story, 1987
AD 三木 健
DE 三木 健
MA 三木 健
CL 三木健デザイン事務所

72
Greeting Card, 1987
AD Ken Miki
DE Ken Miki
MA Ken Miki
CL Ken Miki Design Office

73

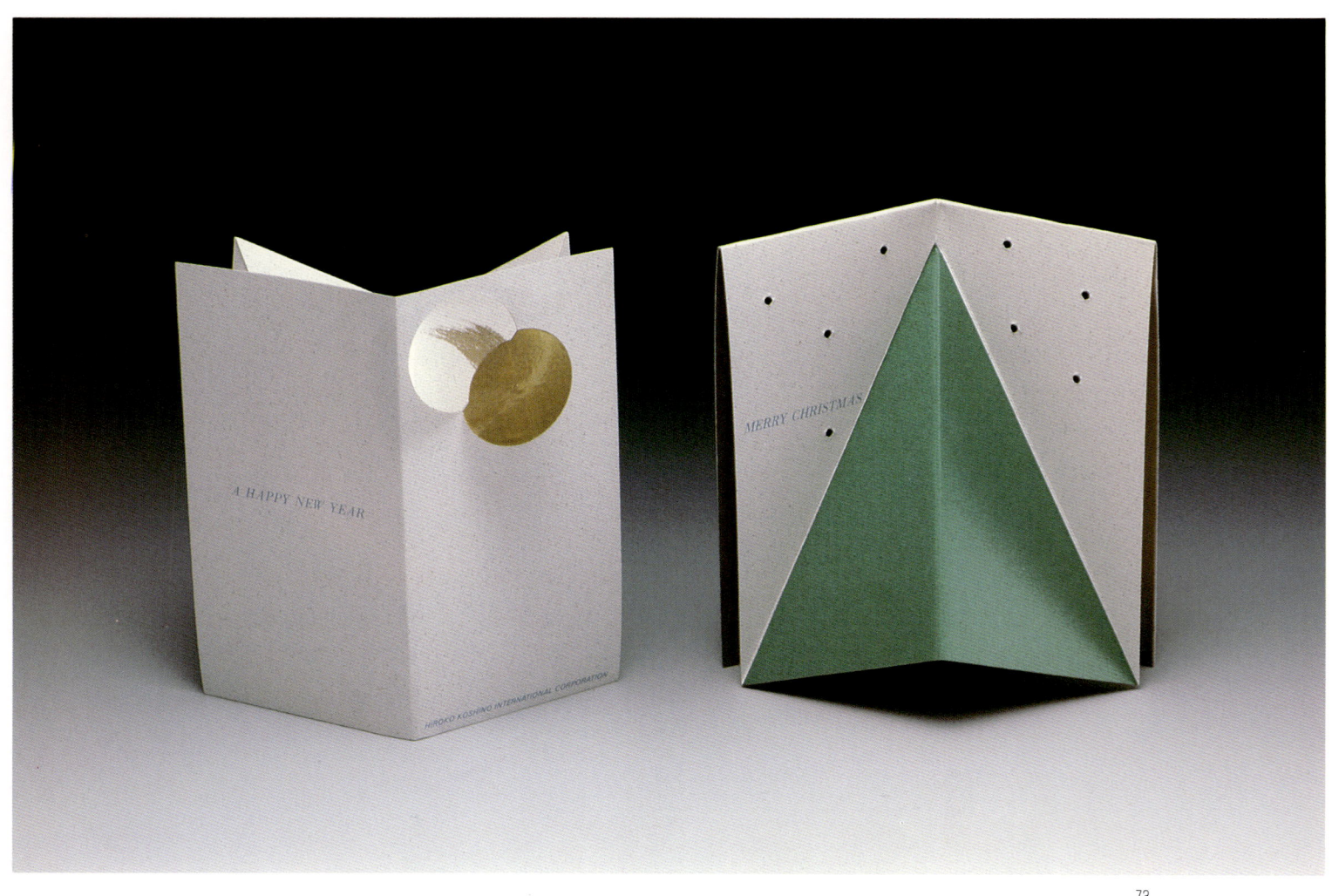

クリスマスカード&年賀状、1987
AD 松井桂三
DE 松井桂三、清水栄治
CN 松井桂三、清水栄治
AG 松井桂三デザイン室
CL ヒロココシノ
　　インターナショナル

73

Christmas and New Year's Card, 1987
AD　Keizo Matsui
DE　Keizo Matsui
　　 Eiji Shimizu
CN　Keizo Matsui
　　 Eiji Shimizu
AG　Keizo Matsu and Associates
CL　Hiroko Koshino International

74a・b

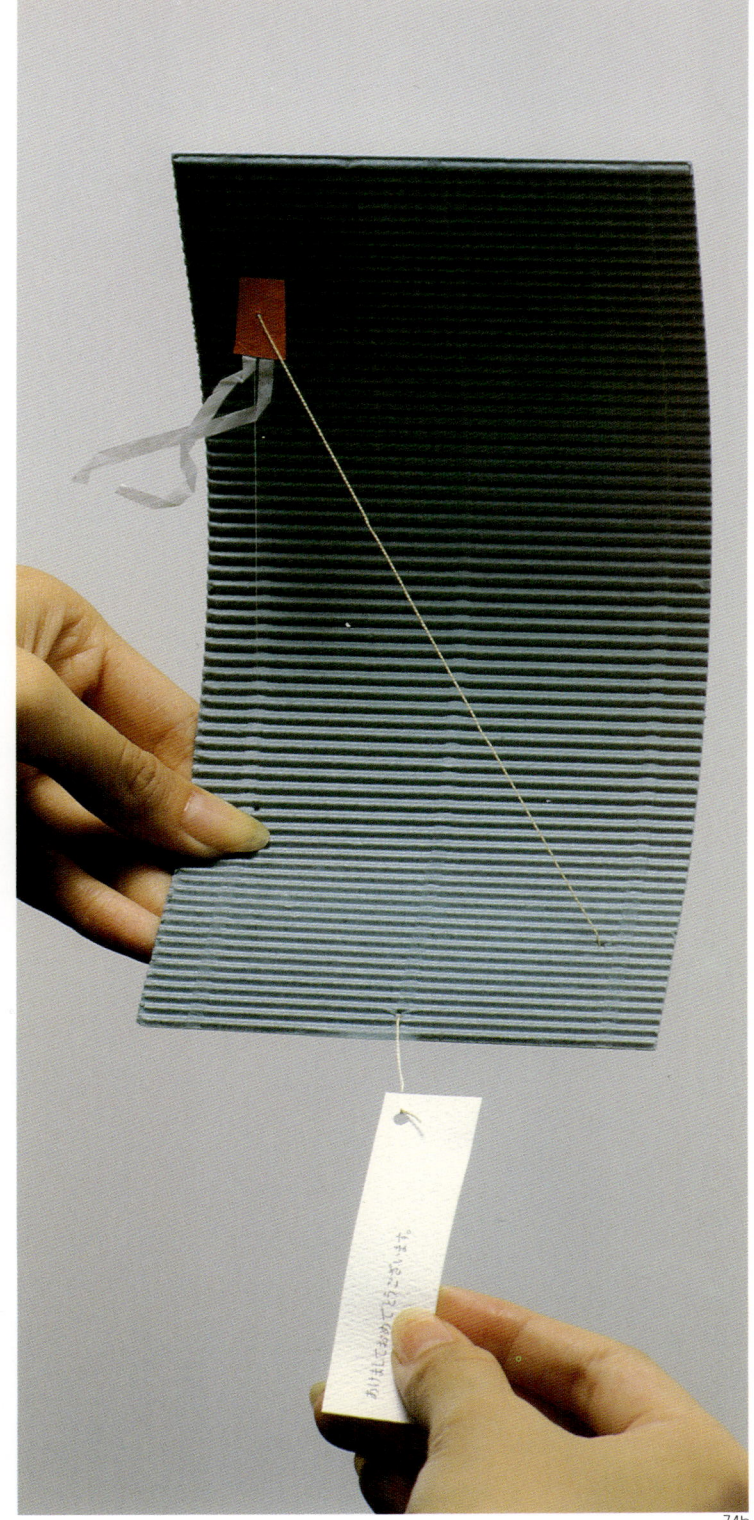

年賀状 凧上げ、1986
AD　松井桂三
DE　松井桂三、清水栄治
CN　松井桂三、清水栄治
CL　松井桂三デザイン室

74a・b

New Year's Card, 1986
AD　Keizo Matsui
DE　Keizo Matsui
　　Eiji Shimizu
CN　Keizo Matsui
　　Eiji Shimizu
CL　Keizo Matsui and
　　Associates

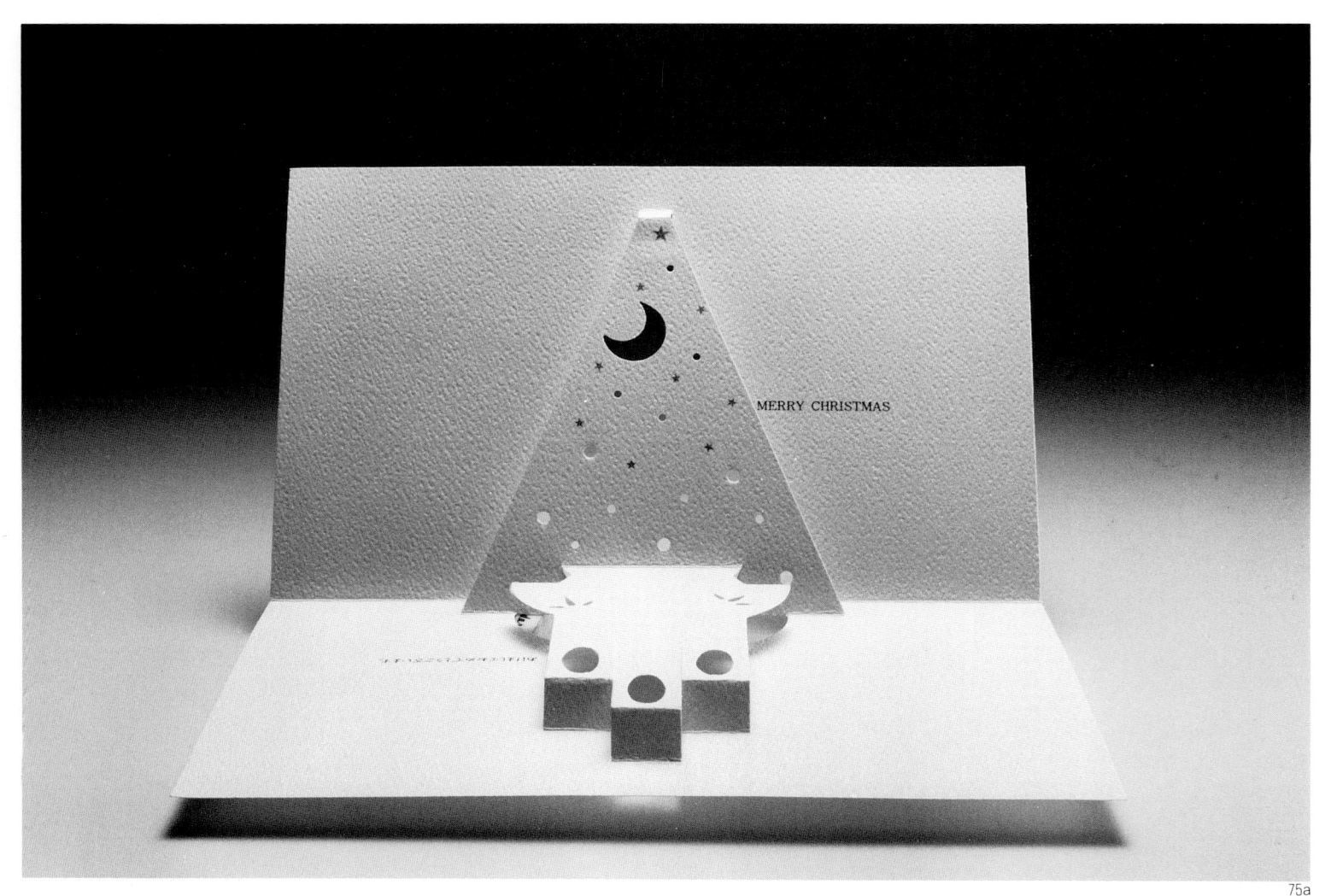

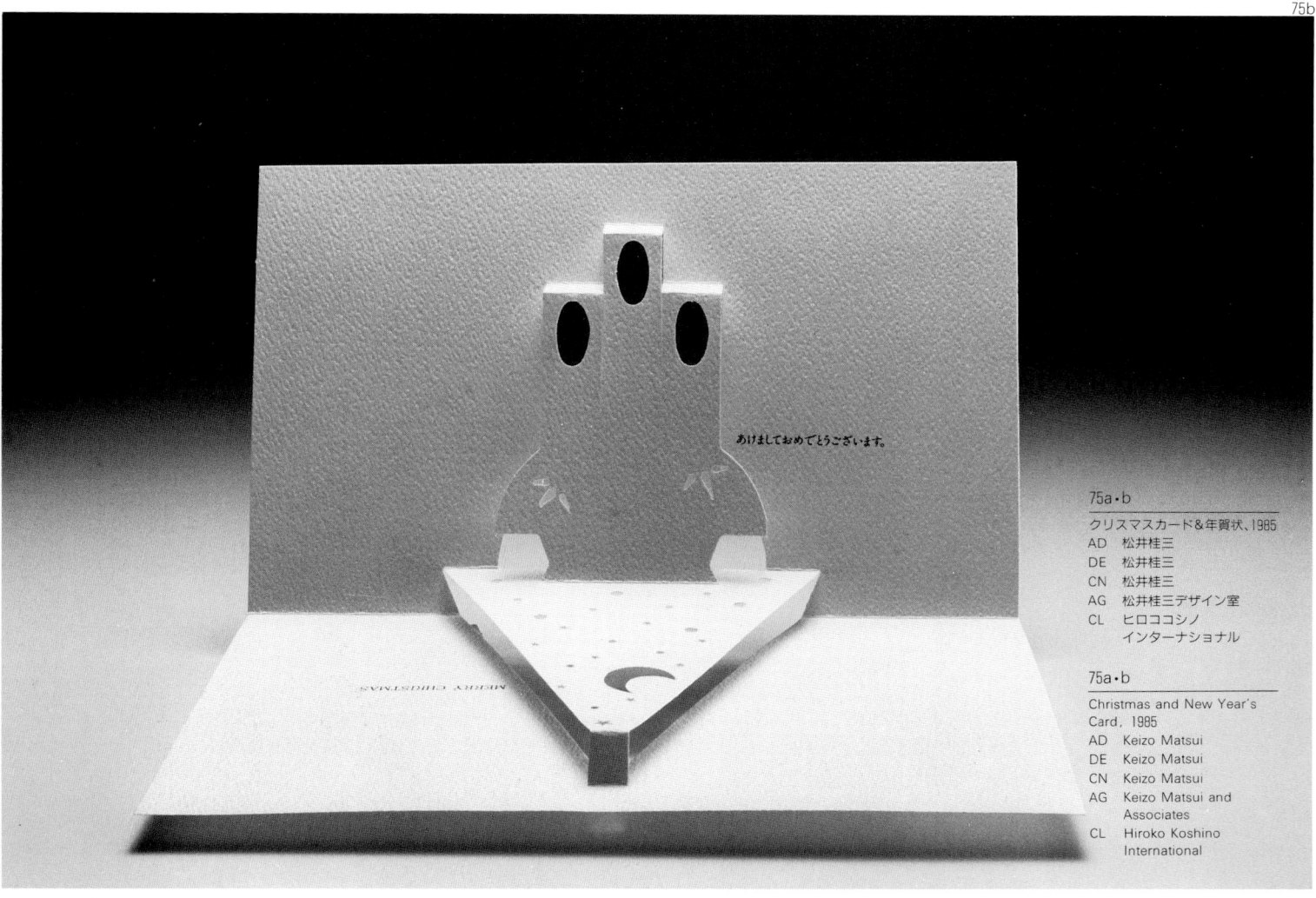

75a·b

クリスマスカード&年賀状、1985
AD　松井桂三
DE　松井桂三
CN　松井桂三
AG　松井桂三デザイン室
CL　ヒロココシノ
　　インターナショナル

75a·b

Christmas and New Year's Card, 1985
AD　Keizo Matsui
DE　Keizo Matsui
CN　Keizo Matsui
AG　Keizo Matsui and Associates
CL　Hiroko Koshino International

76a・b

バースデーカード、1986
AD 松井桂三
DE 松井桂三、清水栄治
CN 松井桂三、清水栄治
CL ヒロココシノ
　　インターナショナル
円の端を回すと、ハッピーバースデーの文字が現われる。

76a・b

Birthday Card, 1986
AD　Keizo Matsui
DE　Keizo Matsui
　　　Eiji Shimizu
CN　Keizo Matsui
　　　Eiji Shimizu
CL　Hiroko Koshino
　　　International
As the circle is turned, "Happy Birthday" appears.

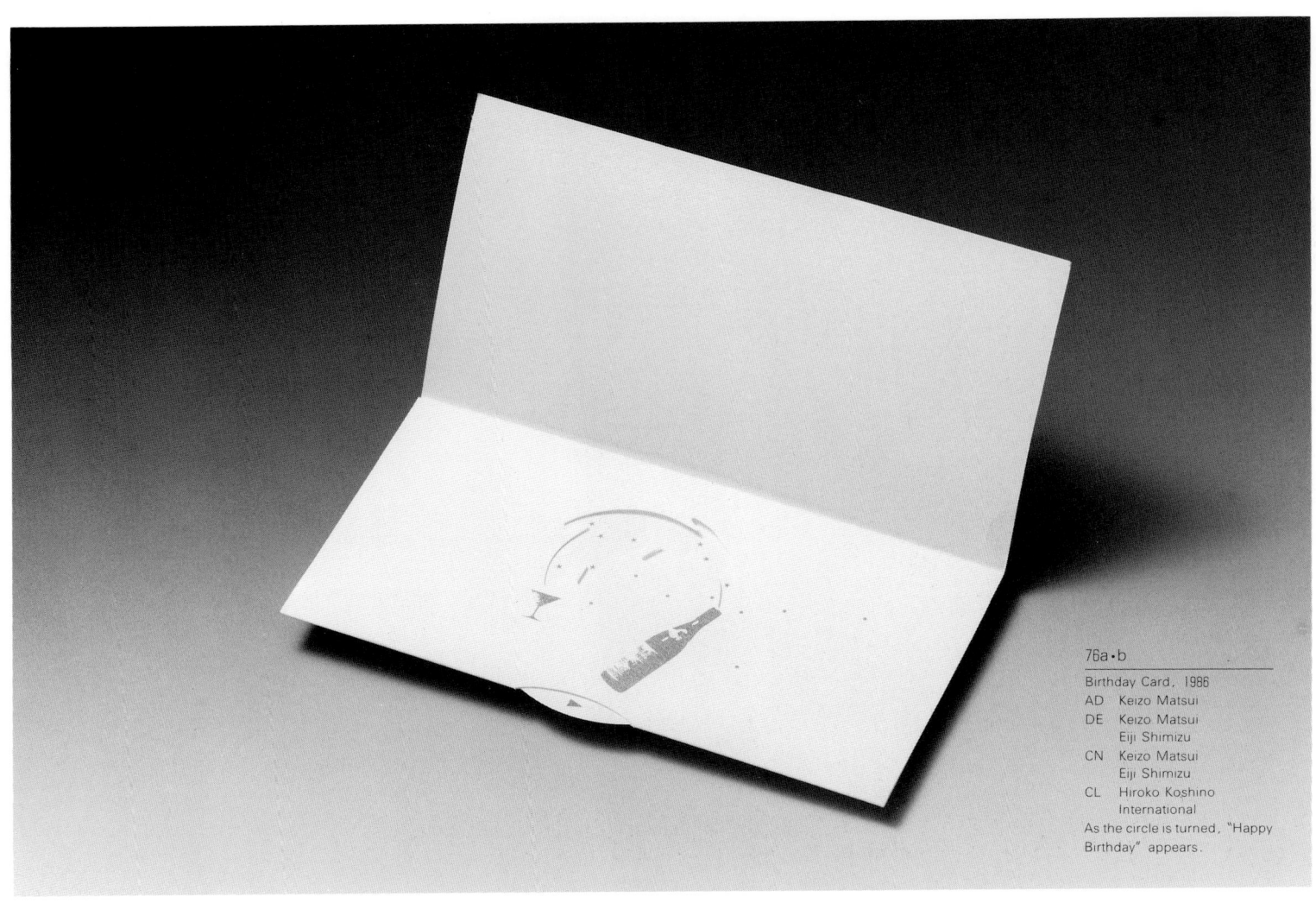

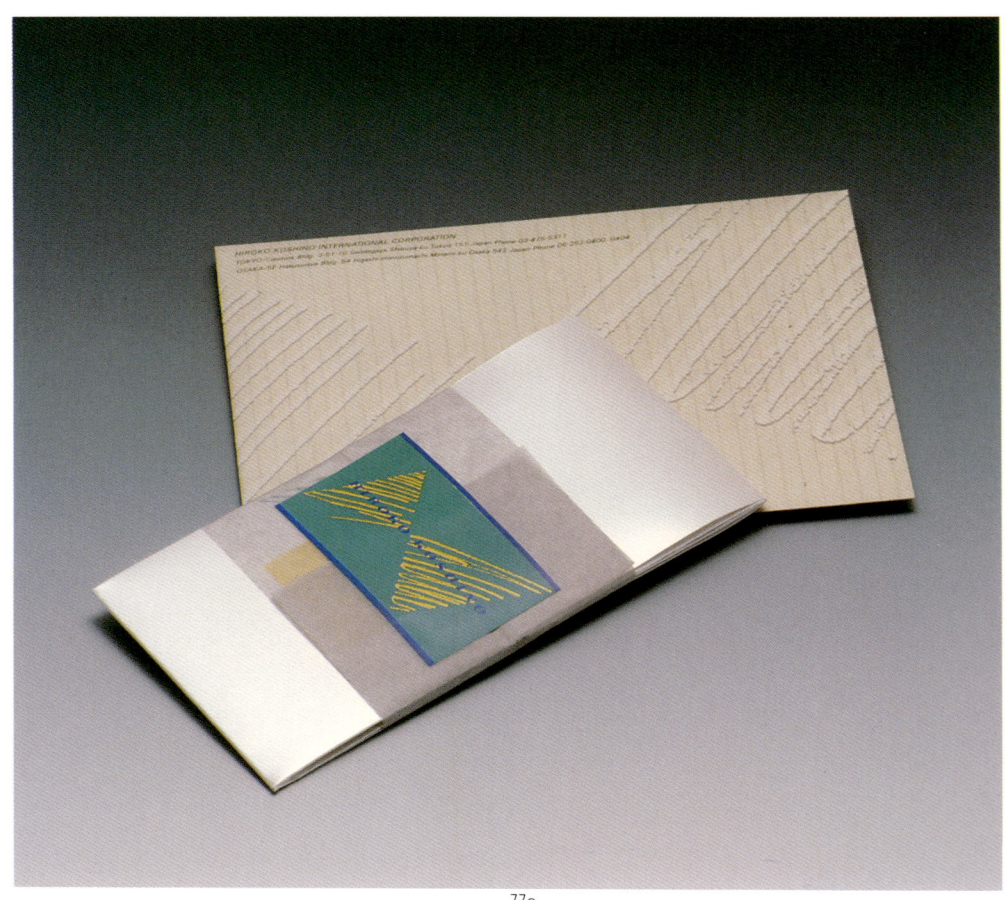

77a

77a・b・c

プレゼントボックス、1987
AD　松井桂三
DE　松井桂三、清水栄治
CN　松井桂三、清水栄治
AG　松井桂三デザイン室
CL　ヒロココシノ
　　インターナショナル
帯を切ると、中からメッセージの書かれた箱が飛び出す。

77a・b・c

Wishes for Birthday, 1987
AD　Keizo Matsui
DE　Keizo Matsui
　　Eiji Shimizu
CN　Keizo Matsui
　　Eiji Shimizu
AG　Keizo Matsui and
　　Associates
CL　Hiroko Koshino
　　International
When unsealed, a box with a message comes out.

77b
77c

97

78

クリスマスカード、1986
AD 氏家嘉子
DE 中沢圭子
CL ギャラリー91（USA）

78

Christmas Card, 1986
AD Yoshiko Ujiie
DE Keiko Nakazawa
CL Gallery 91, New York

79

クリスマスカード、1982
DE 田代耕司

79

Christmas Card, 1982
DE Koji Tashiro

80

スタンディングカード、1985
DE　柿本博康
MA　はいづか印刷
CL　ギャラリー
　　　インターフォーム

80

Christmas Card, 1985
DE　Hiroyasu Kakimoto
MA　Haizuka Printing
CL　Gallery Interform

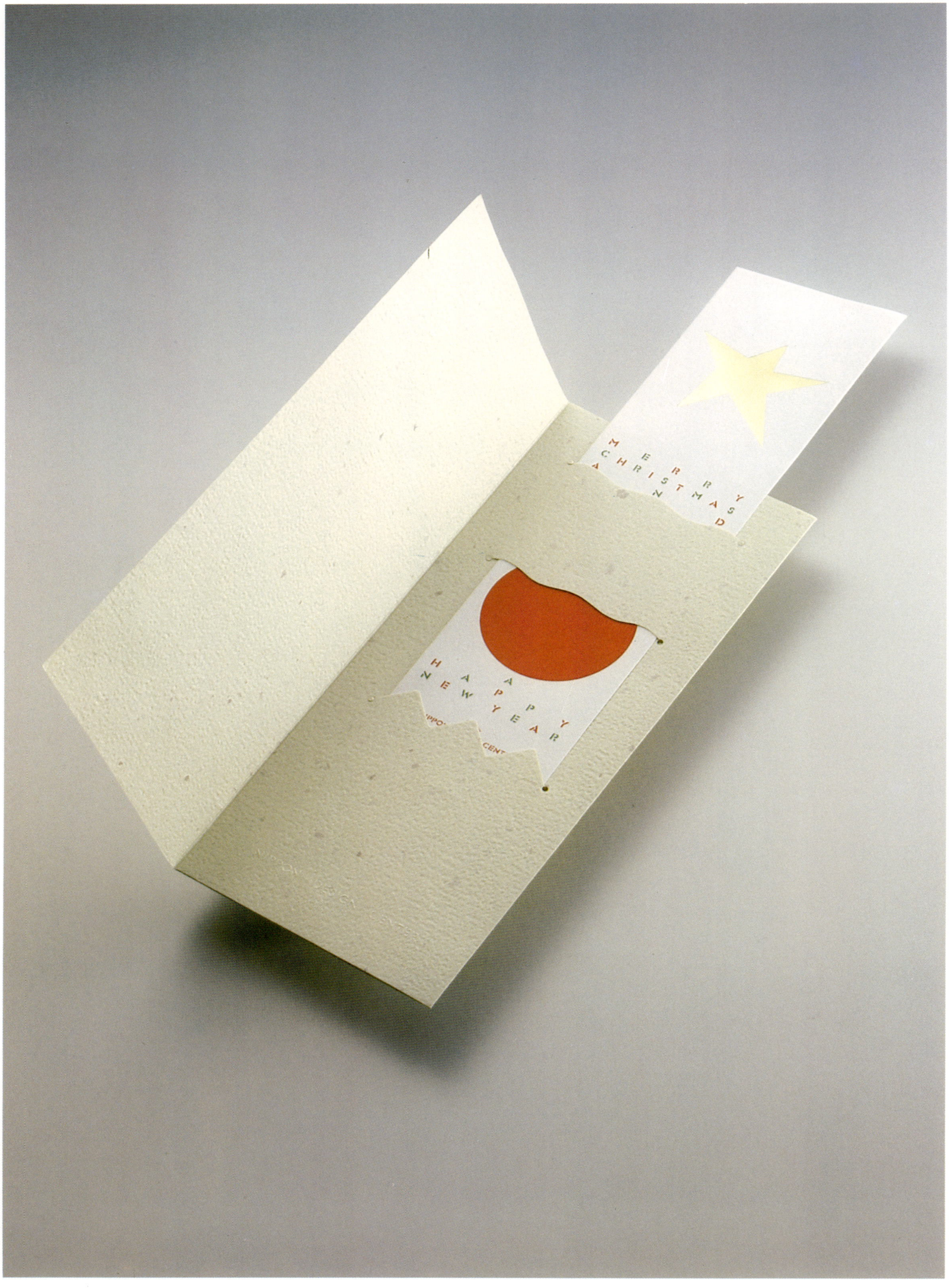
MERRY
CHRISTMAS
AND
HAPPY
NEW YEAR

81

海外向けグリーティングカード、
1986
AD　中川憲造
DE　延山博保、森上 暁
MA　望月印刷
CL　日本デザインセンター
はめ込みの紙を引くと、星と太陽
が現われる。

81

Greeting Card, 1986
AD　Kenzo Nakagawa
DE　Hiroyasu Nobuyama
　　Satoshi Morikami
MA　Mochizuki Printing
CL　Nippon Design Center
When the inserted paper is pulled, a star and the sun appear.

82a・b

展覧会案内状、1986
AD　中川憲造
DE　森上 暁
IL　延山博保
WR　仲畑貴志
MA　望月印刷
CL　東京デザイナーズ
　　スペース
年末の「クリスマス展」と年始の
「年賀状展」という開催時期の異
なる催事告知を1枚ものにした案
内状。それ自体もグリーティングカ
ードに仕立ててある。

82a・b

Invitation to Exhibition, 1986
AD　Kenzo Nakagawa
DE　Satoshi Morikami
IL　Hiroyasu Nobuyama
WR　Takashi Nakahata
MA　Mochizuki Printing
CL　Tokyo Designers Space
An invitation card to "Christmas Exhibition" at the end of the year and "New Year's Card" Exhibition at the beginning of the coming year in one letter. It also serves as a greeting card.

83

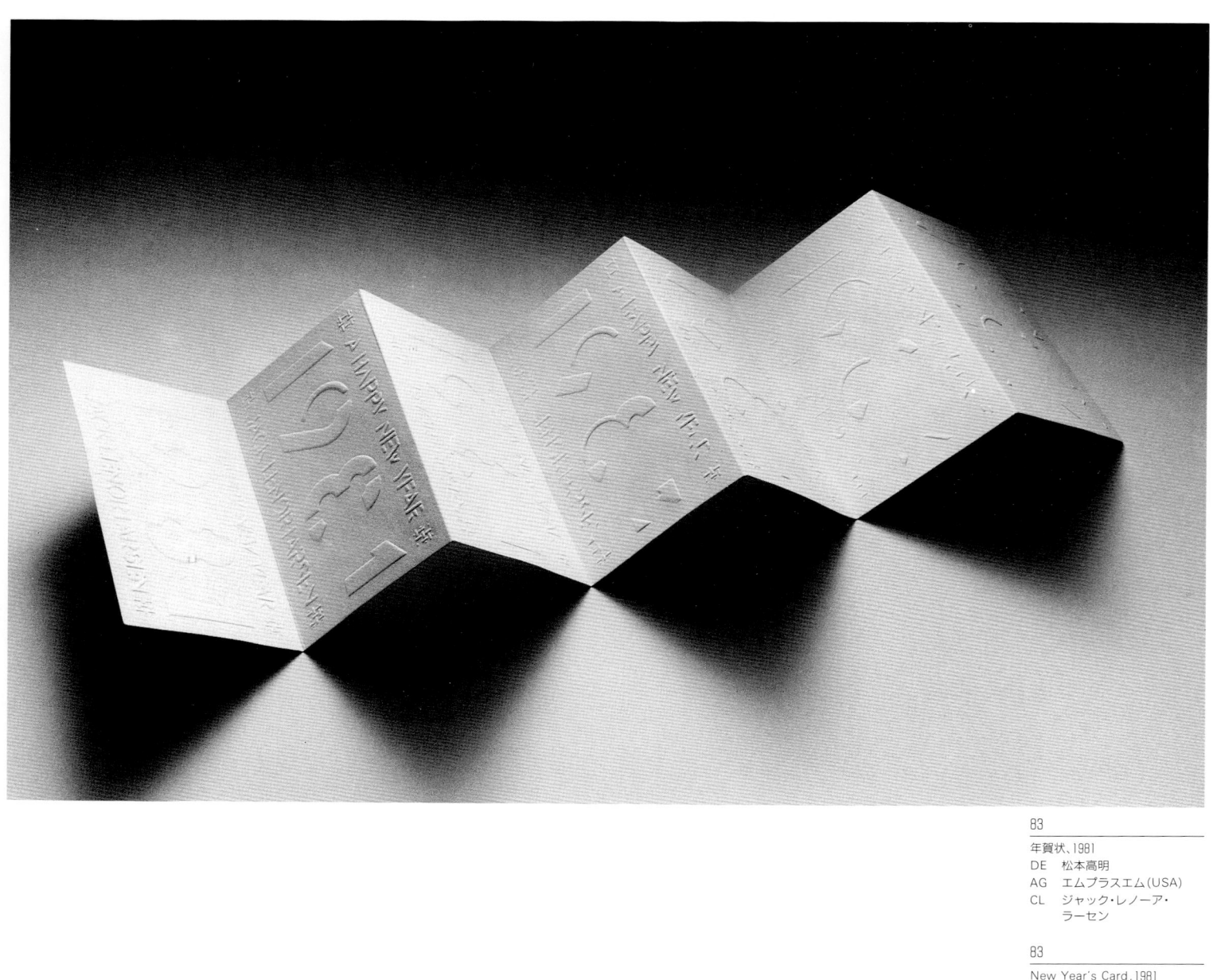

年賀状、1981
DE 松本高明
AG エムプラスエム (USA)
CL ジャック・レノーア・
　　ラーセン

83

New Year's Card, 1981
DE Takaaki Matsumoto
AG M Plus M, New York
CL Jack Lenor Larsen

84

クリスマスカード、1983
DE　田代耕司

84

Christmas Card, 1983
DE　Koji Tashiro

86
年賀状 1984、1985
DE 勝井三雄

86
New Year's Card 1984、1985
DE Mitsuo Katsui

87
グリーティングカード、1987
DE 勝井三雄

87
Greeting Card, 1987
DE Mitsuo Katsui

85

85
サントリーホール"響"、1986
AD 三木 健
DE 三木 健
MA 三木 健
CL サントリーホール
1枚の紙でできている折りたためる箱型カード。試作。

85
Greeting Card, 1986
AD Ken Miki
DE Ken Miki
MA Ken Miki
CL Suntory Hall
A box-type card made of a strip of paper. Flattened to put into an envelope. A trial.

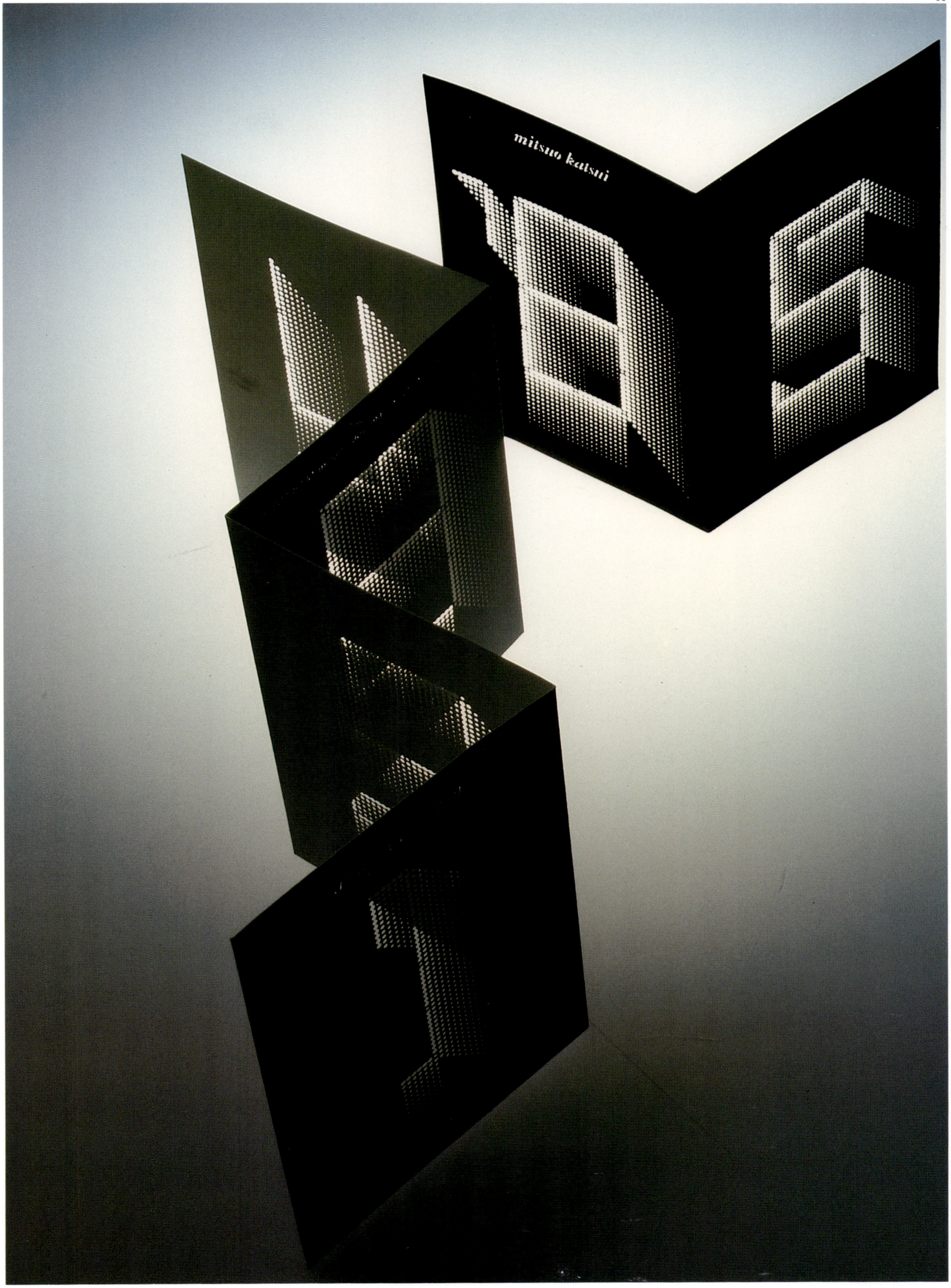
mitsuo katsui

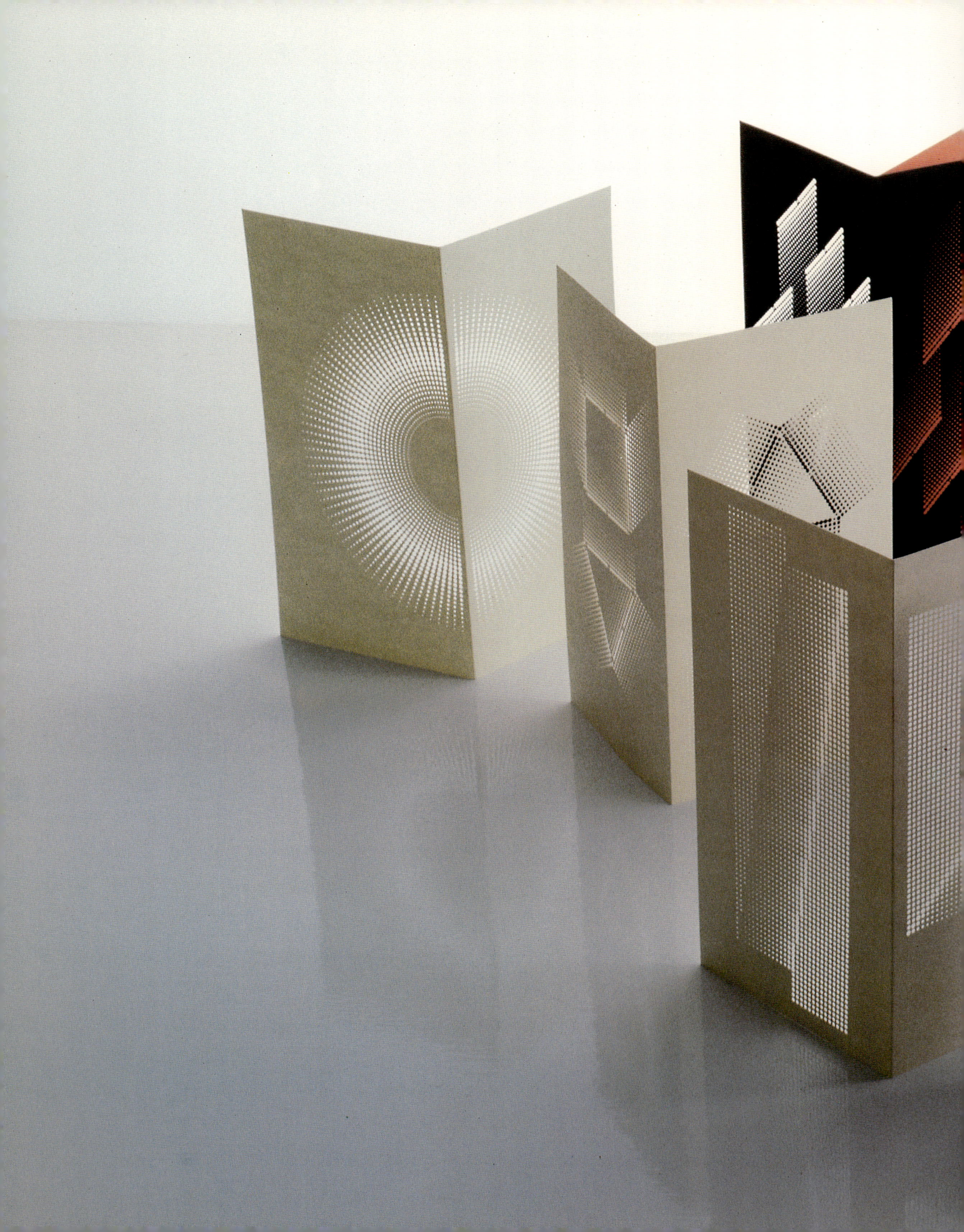

87

88
アンリシャルパンティエ
バースデーカード、1977
DE　森島 紘
WR　蟻田善造
CL　アンリシャルパンティエ
紙風船入りの洋菓子屋からの誕生
日祝いカード

88
Birthday Card, 1977
DE　Hiroshi Morishima
WR　Zenzo Arita
CL　Henri Charpentier
A birthday card from a cake shop containing a folded paper baloon

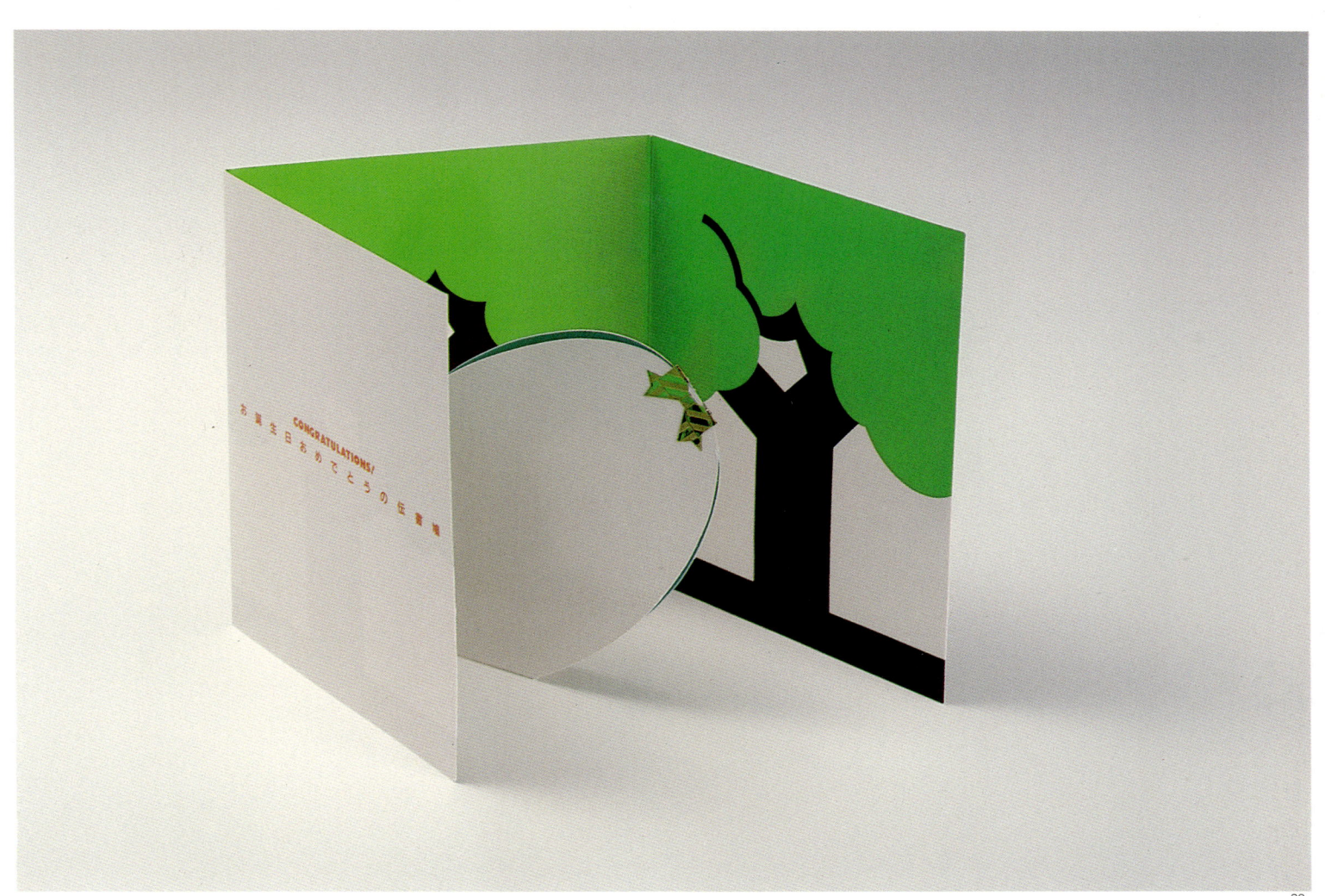

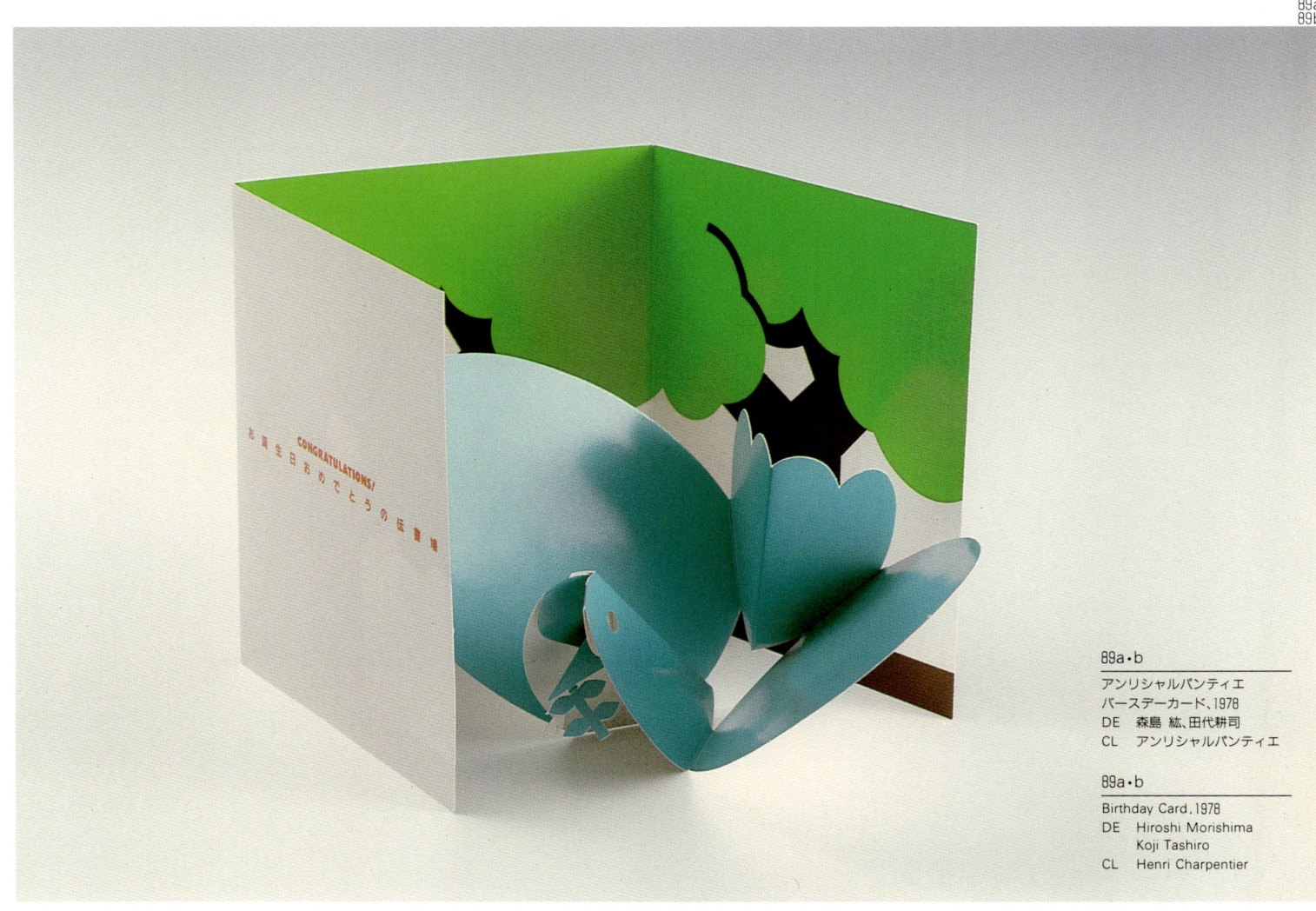

89a·b

アンリシャルパンティエ
バースデーカード, 1978
DE　森島 紘、田代耕司
CL　アンリシャルパンティエ

89a·b

Birthday Card, 1978
DE　Hiroshi Morishima
　　 Koji Tashiro
CL　Henri Charpentier

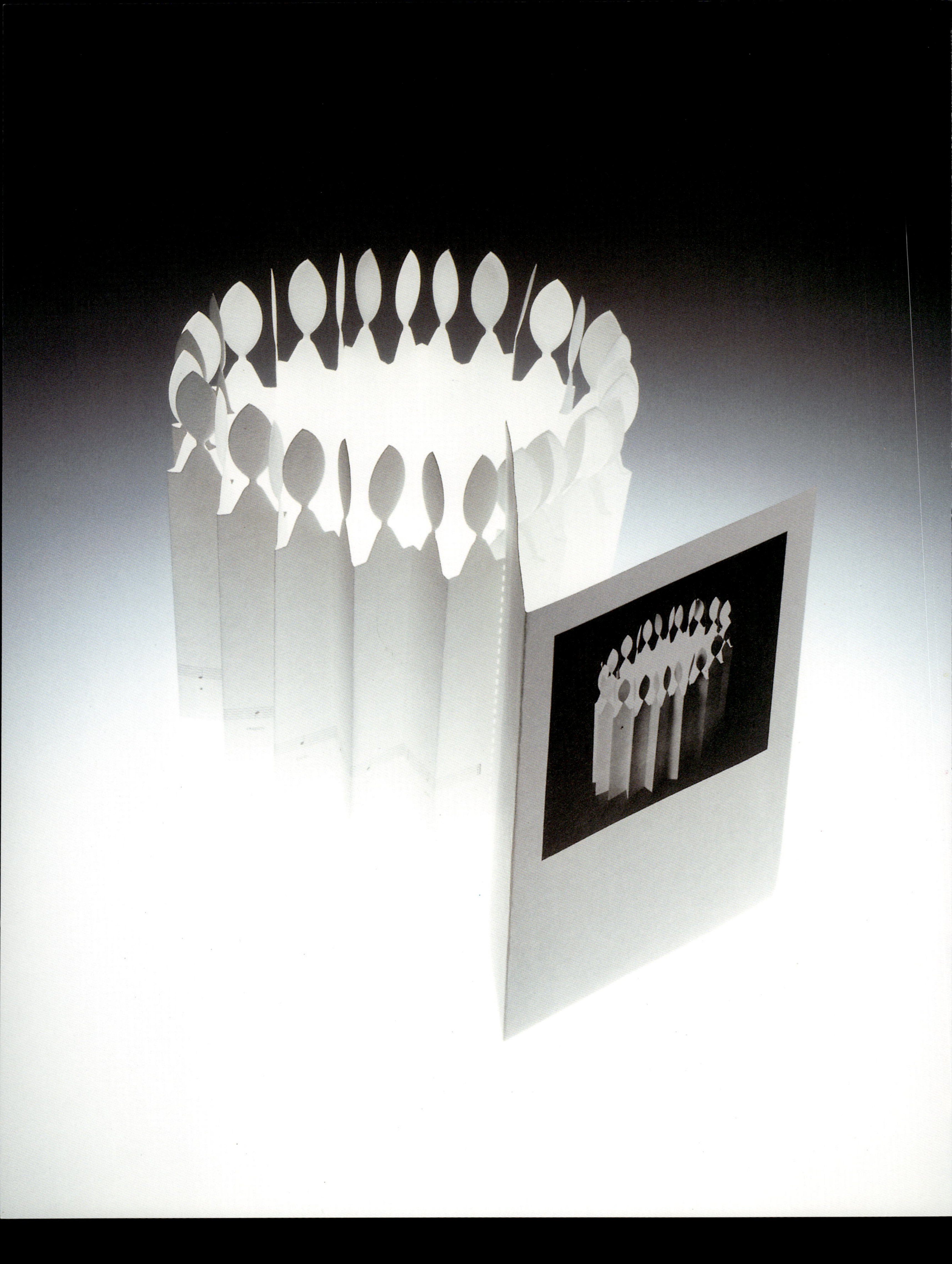

90b

90a・b

バースデーカード、1979
DE 森島 紘
ろうそくの下部に、ハッピーバースデーのメロディが印刷されている。

90a・b

Birthday Card, 1979
DE　Hiroshi Morishima
The score of "Happy Birthday to You" is printed on the lower part of the candle.

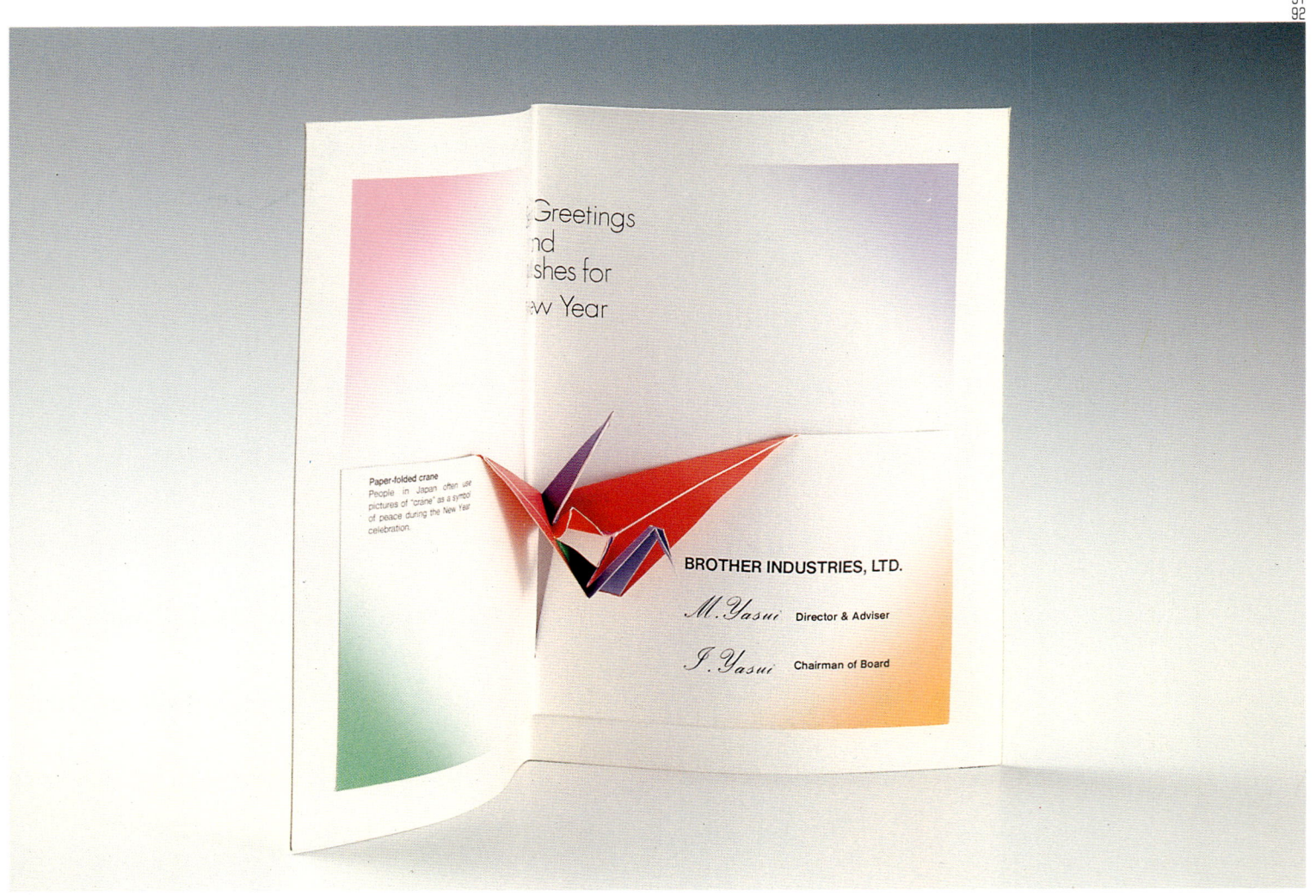

Season's Greetings and Best Wishes for The New Year

Battledore and shuttlecock
During the New Year season, Japanese girls play "battledore and shuttlecock" or display them in the living room.

BROTHER INDUSTRIES, LTD.

H. NAKAOKI — Director
T. KANEKO — Manager
T. UTSUMI — Manager

Paper-folded crane
People in Japan often use pictures of "crane" as a symbol of peace during the New Year celebration.

BROTHER INDUSTRIES, LTD.

M. Yasui — Director & Adviser
J. Yasui — Chairman of Board

91・92
ブラザー海外向けクリスマスカード、
1986
DE　杉井清二
MA　杉井清二
CL　ブラザー工業

91・92
Christmas Card, 1986
DE　Seiji Sugii
MA　Seiji Sugii
CL　Brother Industries

93
HUSTLE'85、1984
DE　杉井清二
MA　杉井清二
CL　杉井デザイン事務所
1本の輪ゴムを使ったポップアップカード

93
HUSTLE'85、1984
DE　Seiji Sugii
MA　Seiji Sugii
CL　Sugii Design Office
A pop-up card using a rubber ring

94

シンバルザル、1980
DE 杉井清二
MA 杉井清二
CL 杉井デザイン事務所
5円玉2個をはさみ、カードを開閉するとシンバルが鳴る。

94

New Year's Card, 1980
DE Seiji Sugii
MA Seiji Sugii
CL Sugii Design Office
As the card is opened and closed, two coins sound like cymbals.

95
HANAE MORIクリスマスカード、
1986
AD　谷内庸生
DE　谷内庸生
MA　東企
CL　オンワード樫山
勢いをつけてカードを開くと、糸でつながれた紙片がまわって、Merry Christmasの文字が現われる。

95
Christmas Card, 1986
AD　Tsuneo Taniuchi
DE　Tsuneo Taniuchi
MA　Toki
CL　Onward Kashiyama
When forced to open, paper pieces tied with a string go around and the letters "Merry Christmas" appear.

POSTERS
CALENDARS
PACKAGING
CATALOGUES
MAGAZINE INSERT
P.O.P. TOOLS
ILLUSTRATIONS
・
ポスター
カレンダー
パッケージ
カタログ
雑誌折込広告
P.O.P.ツール
イラストレーション

ダイカットカード、1984
DE　マリオ・アルメンゴル
CL　ギャラリー・ファイブ（イギリス）

Die Cut Card, 1984
DE　Mario Armengol
CL　Gallery Five, London

幸運は各駅停車。サントリーオールド

車内初詣。

96
車内初詣、1984
PL/PR オリコミ
AD 松本和夫
DE 松本和夫
WR 奈良坂 進
MA 東洋紙業
CL サントリー

96
Hanger in a Train, 1984
PL/PR Orikomi
AD Kazuo Matsumoto
DE Kazuo Matsumoto
WR Susumu Narasaka
MA Toyo Shigyo Printing
CL Suntory

97
車内吊り広告'おみくじ'、1985
PL/PR オリコミ
CD 千葉孝義
AD 穐田 貢
DE 小松原正光
WR 市川 隆,殿岡 紀
MA 東洋紙業
CL サントリー

97
Hanger in a Train, 1985
PL/PR Orikomi
CD Takayoshi Chiba
AD Mitsugu Akita
DE Masamitsu Komatsubara
WR Takashi Ichikawa
   Hajime Tonooka
MA Toyo Shigyo Printing
CL Suntory

年の始めの縁結び。

TDS新推人薦展
4月1日(火)〜7月26日(土)
東京デザイナーズスペース
(AXISビル4階 午後12時〜7時/日・祝はお休み)
イラストレーション❶ 4月1日(火)〜4月12日(土)
イラストレーション❷ 4月15日(火)〜4月26日(土)
イラストレーション❸ 5月6日(火)〜5月17日(土)
グラフィック❶ 5月20日(火)〜5月31日(土)
グラフィック❷ 6月3日(火)〜6月14日(土)
写真・CG・ビデオ 6月17日(火)〜6月28日(土)
プロダクト・立体 7月1日(火)〜7月12日(土)
From N.Y. 7月15日(火)〜7月26日(土)
TOKYO
DESIGNERS
SPACE

Geigy Graphics on exhibition april 1967
princeton university   school of architecture

99a

Geigy Graphics on exhibition april 1967
princeton university   school of architecture

99b

98
東京デザイナーズスペース
新人展ポスター、1986
AD 中川憲造
DE 森上 暁
IL 延山博保
WR 仲畑貴志
MA 光村オフセット印刷
CL 東京デザイナーズ
　　スペース
ブック・マッチ型のポスター。壁に貼ると、マッチの頭が前傾する。

98
Poster, 1986
AD Kenzo Nakagawa
DE Satoshi Morikami
IL Hiroyasu Nobuyama
WR Takashi Nakahata
MA Mitsumura Offset
　　Printing
CL Tokyo Designers Space
A book match type poster. The "matches" move when hung on the wall.

99a・b
ゲイジーポスター、1967
AD エミリオ・アンバース
DE エミリオ・アンバース
PR ゲイジーケミカル
MA ジーン・フェルドマン/
　　ファルコン・プレス(USA)
CL プリンストン大学(USA)
Gの文字をおこして、いろいろなパターンにアレンジすることができる。

99a・b
Poster, 1967
AD Emilio Ambasz
DE Emilio Ambasz
PR Geigy Chemical
MA Gene Feldman/Falcon
　　Press, Philadelphia, USA
CL Princeton University,
　　New Jersey, USA
Large letter G dye-cut for a 2 inch-strip can be rearranged in different three-dimensional configurations.

100
「World Man: Bucky Fuller」展
ポスター、1966
DE エミリオ・アンバース
PR M.ローレタノ
CL プリンストン大学(USA)
メタリック・ペーパーを折り重ね、フラーの提唱した三次元的構造(ジオデシック構造)を想起させる円をつくった。

100
Poster, 1966
DE Emilio Ambasz
PR M. Lauretano
CL Princeton University,
　　New Jersey, USA
Heavy metallized paper stock is folded and the two dye-cut concentric rings are folded so as to conform a three-dimensional construction in an image of Fuller's geodesic structure.

world man   bucky fuller

mc cosh 10
october 5
8 p. m.

princeton university   school of architecture

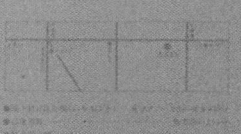

EMILIO AMBASZ
ARCHITECTURAL · INDUSTRIAL · GRAPHIC · EXHIBIT DESIGN

101	101	102	102
アンバース展ポスター、1985	Poster, 1985	Surface & Ornament ポスター、1982	Poster, 1982
AD エミリオ・アンバース	AD Emilio Ambasz	AD エミリオ・アンバース	AD Emilio Ambasz
DE エミリオ・アンバース	DE Emilio Ambasz	DE エミリオ・アンバース カレン・スケルトン	DE Emilio Ambasz Karen Skelton
MA 大日本印刷	MA Dai Nippon Printing	CL フォーマイカ(USA)	CL Formica, New Jersey, USA
CL アクシス	CL Axis	フォーマイカ社の製品「カラーコア」化粧板の特性を表現した三次元的ポスター	A three-dimensional poster expressing the characteristics of "Color Core"(a smoothly planed board), a Formica's product

木 H. I. R. O. K. O.

103・104
ヒロコオム ポスター、1987
AD 松井桂三
DE 松井桂三、長尾仁美、
   清水栄治
PH 村上ひろし
CL ヒロココシノ
   インターナショナル

103・104
Poster for Hiroko Homme, 1987
AD Keizo Matsui
DE Keizo Matsui, Hitomi Nagao, Eiji Shimizu
PH Hiroshi Murakami
CL Hiroko Koshino International

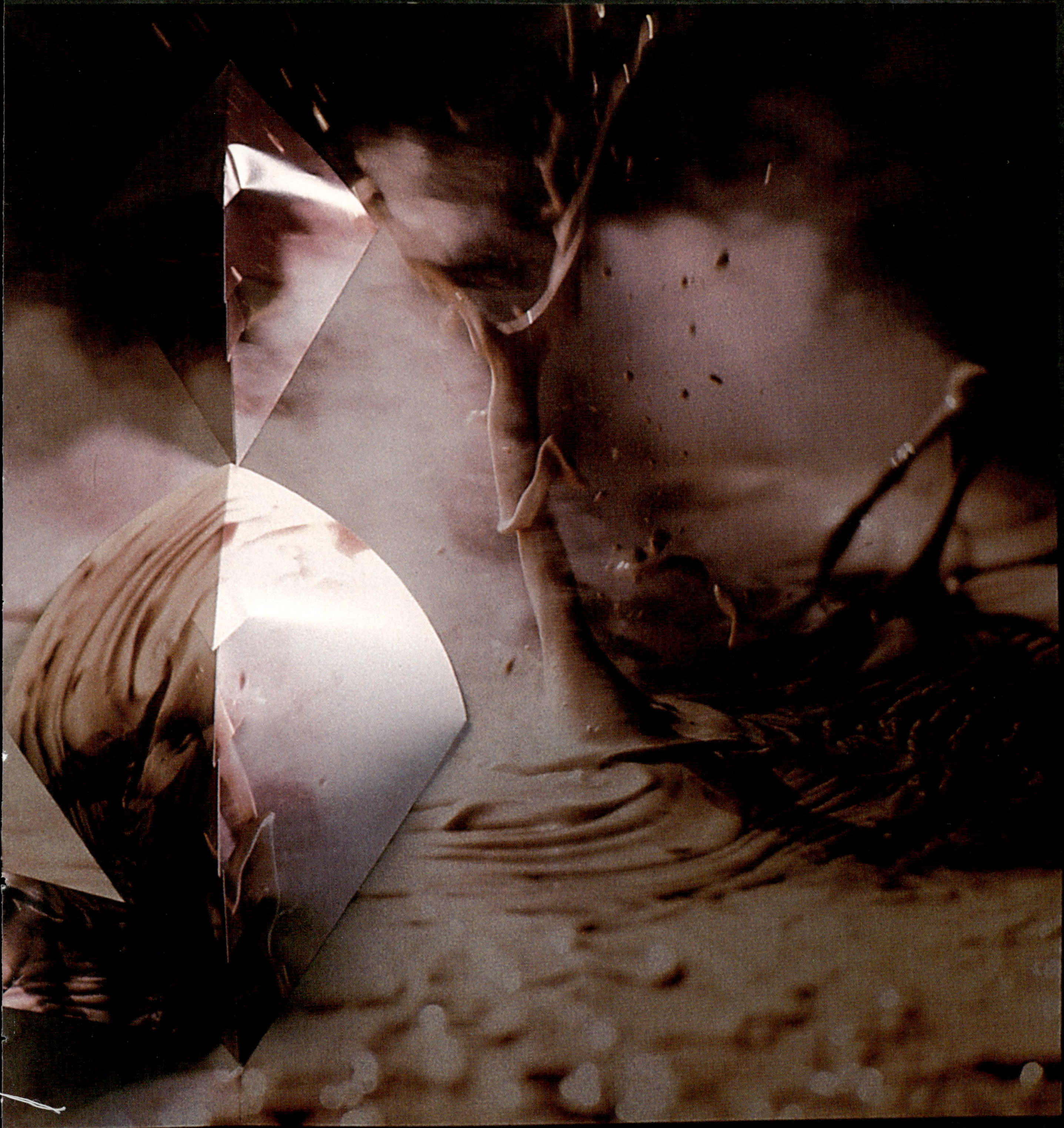

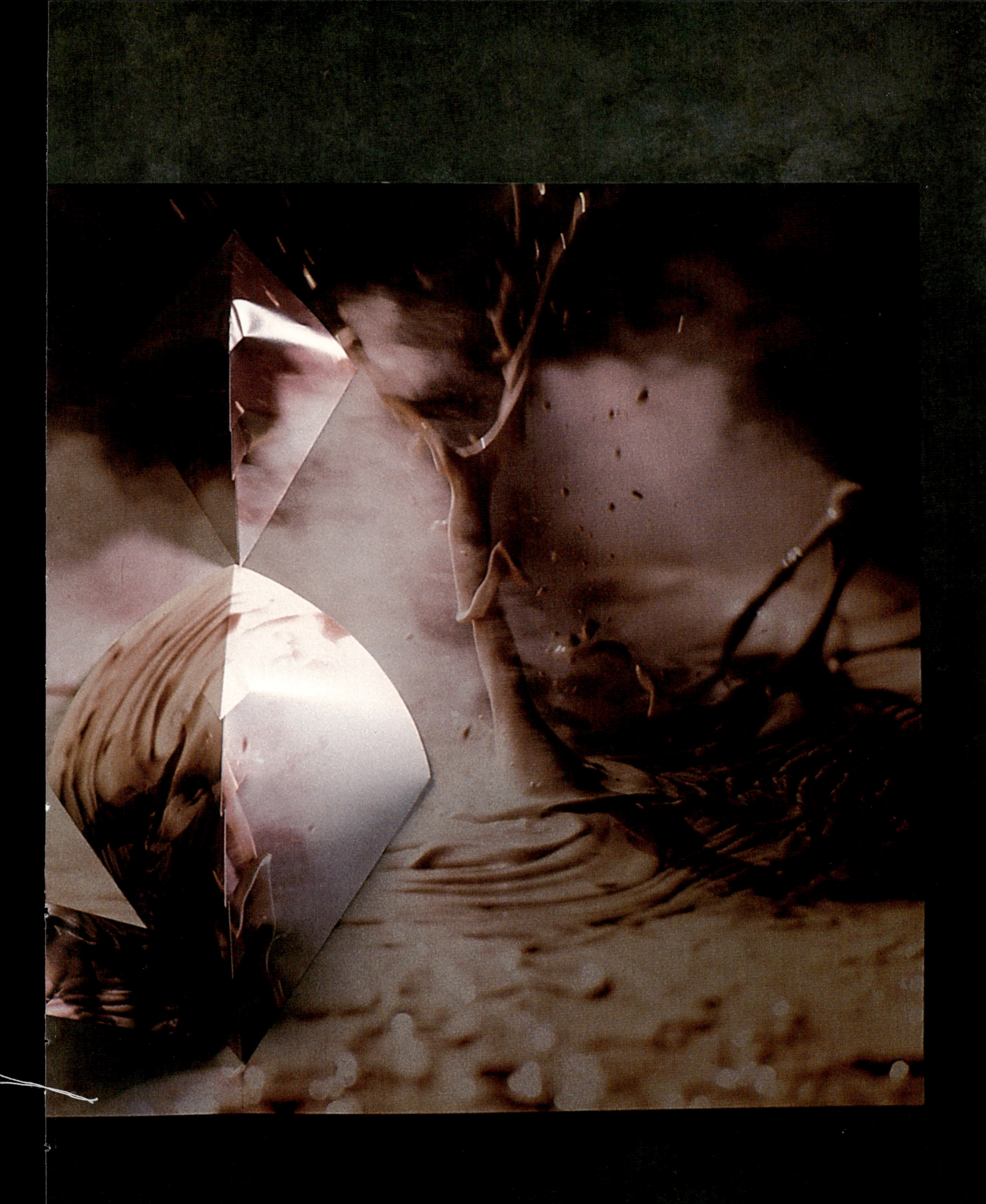

105

105

カレンダー、1986
DE　ジョイス・カルキン
CN　ジョイス・カルキン
CL　ビットストリーム(USA)
Digital Type Design Company
のためにつくられたプロモーション用カレンダー

105

Promotional Calendar, 1986
DE　Joyce Culkin
CN　Joyce Culkin
CL　Bitstream, Boston, USA
Promotional Calendar for Digital Type Design Company

Bitstream
S M T W T F S
1
2 3 4 5 6 7 8
9 10 11 12 13 14 15
16 17 18 19 20 21 22
23 24 25 26 27 28
February

S M T W T F S
1 2 3 4 5
6 7 8 9 10 11 12
13 14 15 16 17 18 19
20 21 22 23 24 25 26
27 28 29 30
April
Bitstream

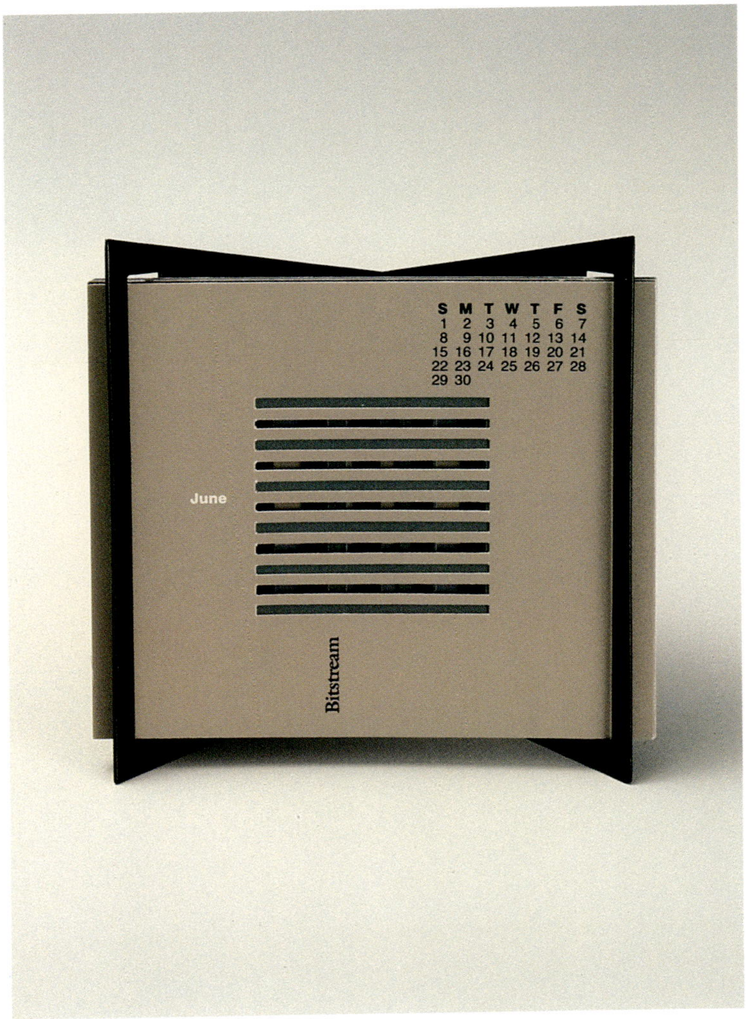
S M T W T F S
1 2 3 4 5 6 7
8 9 10 11 12 13 14
15 16 17 18 19 20 21
22 23 24 25 26 27 28
29 30
June
Bitstream

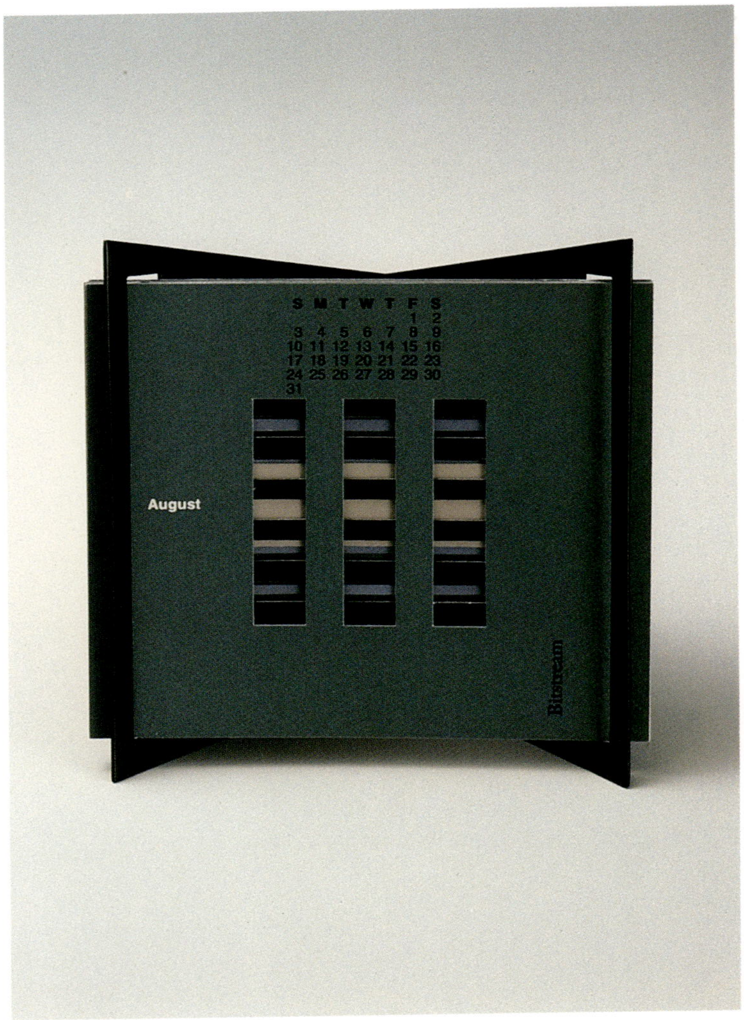
S M T W T F S
1 2
3 4 5 6 7 8 9
10 11 12 13 14 15 16
17 18 19 20 21 22 23
24 25 26 27 28 29 30
31
August
Bitstream

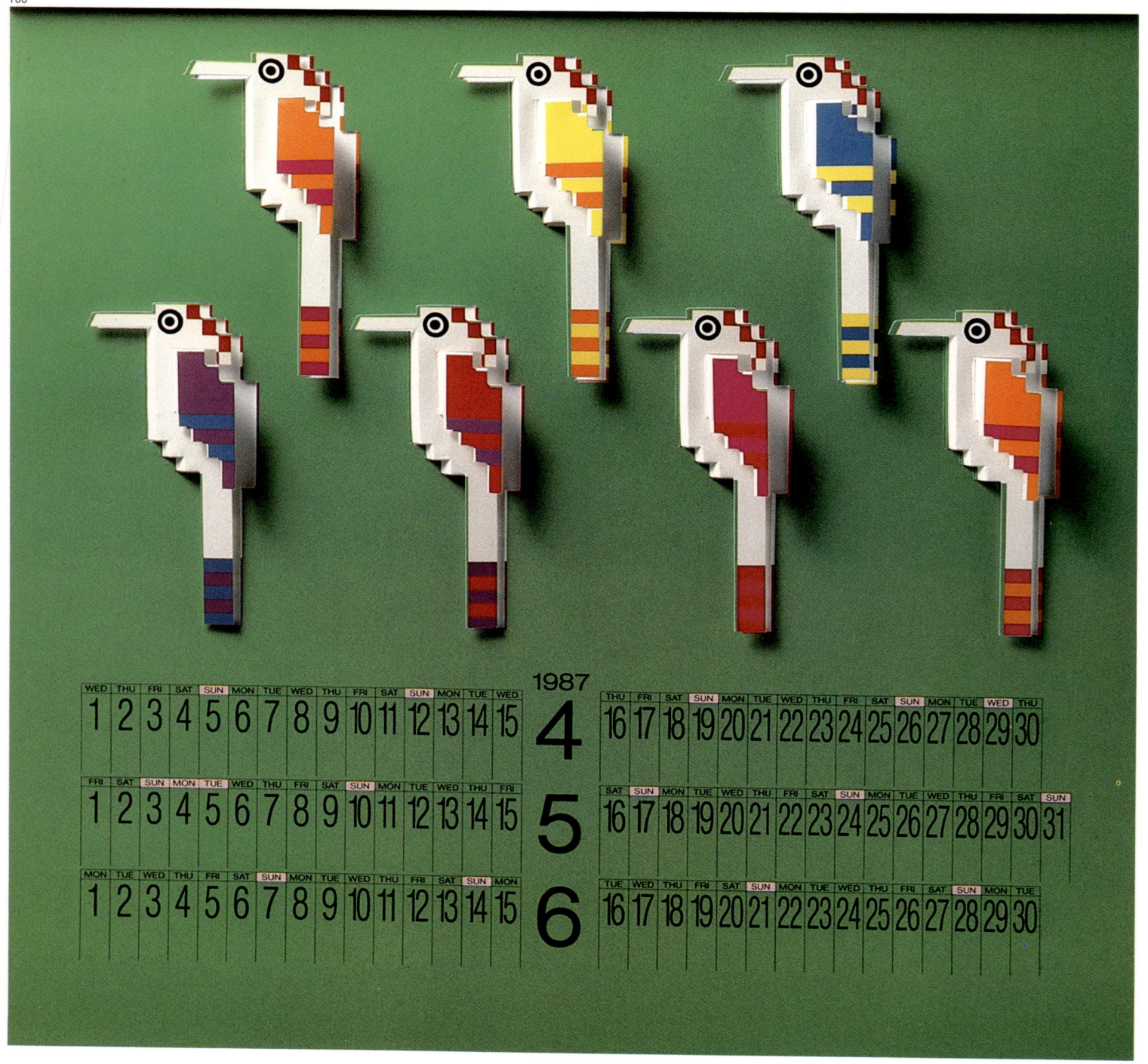

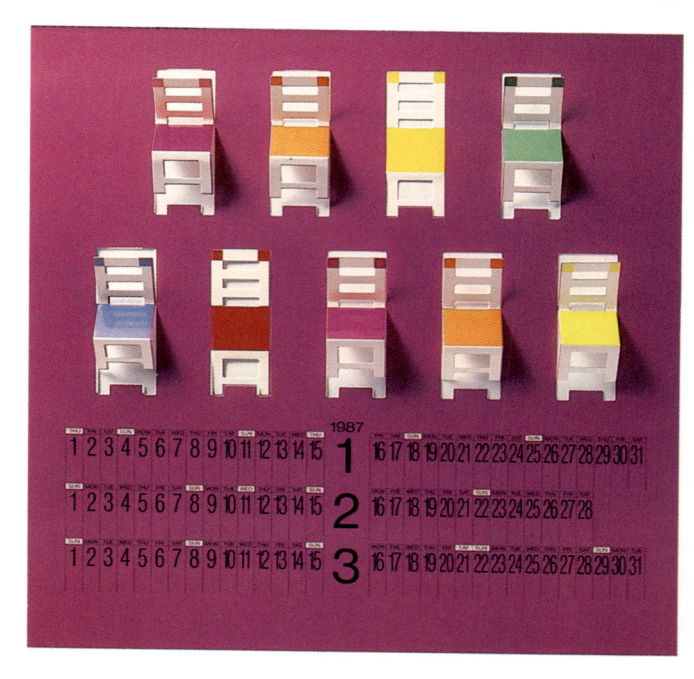

WED	THU	FRI	SAT	SUN	MON	TUE	WED	THU	FRI	SAT	SUN	MON	TUE	WED	1987	THU	FRI	SAT	SUN	MON	TUE	WED	THU	FRI	SAT	SUN	MON	TUE	WED	THU
1	2	3	4	5	6	7	8	9	10	11	12	13	14	15	**4**	16	17	18	19	20	21	22	23	24	25	26	27	28	29	30

FRI	SAT	SUN	MON	TUE	WED	THU	FRI	SAT	SUN	MON	TUE	WED	THU	FRI		SAT	SUN	MON	TUE	WED	THU	FRI	SAT	SUN	MON	TUE	WED	THU	FRI	SAT	SUN
1	2	3	4	5	6	7	8	9	10	11	12	13	14	15	**5**	16	17	18	19	20	21	22	23	24	25	26	27	28	29	30	31

MON	TUE	WED	THU	FRI	SAT	SUN	MON	TUE	WED	THU	FRI	SAT	SUN	MON		TUE	WED	THU	FRI	SAT	SUN	MON	TUE	WED	THU	FRI	SAT	SUN	MON	TUE
1	2	3	4	5	6	7	8	9	10	11	12	13	14	15	**6**	16	17	18	19	20	21	22	23	24	25	26	27	28	29	30

106

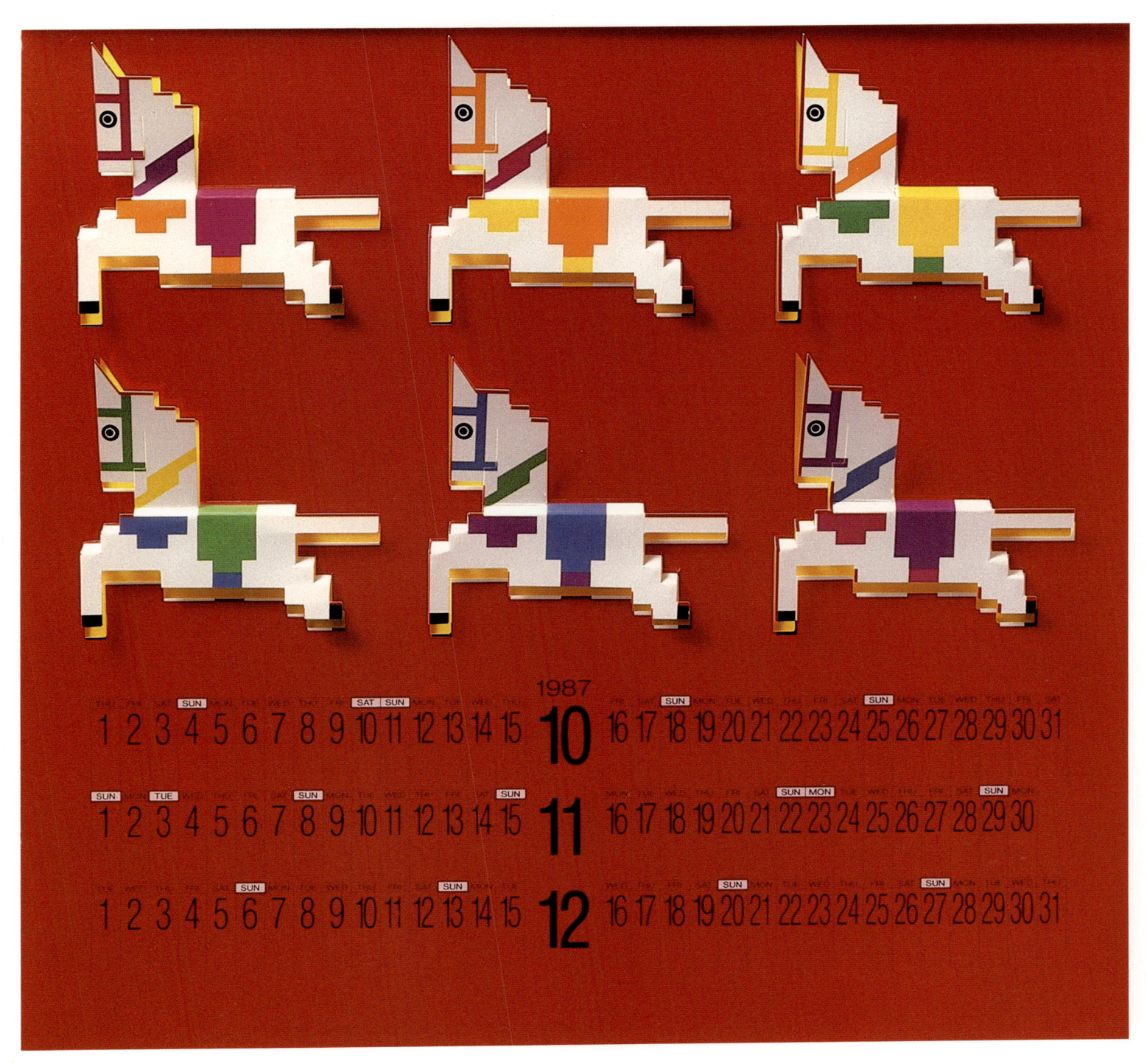

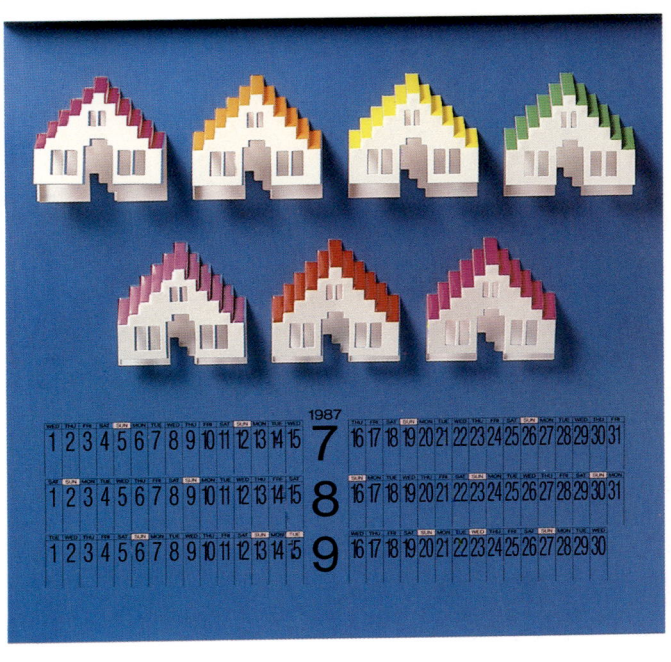

Paper Construction, 1986
AD 杉井清二
DE 杉井清二
CN 杉井清二
CL 杉井デザイン事務所

106

Calendar, 1986
AD Seiji Sugii
DE Seiji Sugii
CN Seiji Sugii
CL Sugii Design Office

107

Paper Construction, 1985
AD 杉井清二
DE 杉井清二
CN 杉井清二
CL 平和紙業

107

Calendar, 1985
AD Seiji Sugii
DE Seiji Sugii
CN Seiji Sugii
CL Heiwa Paper

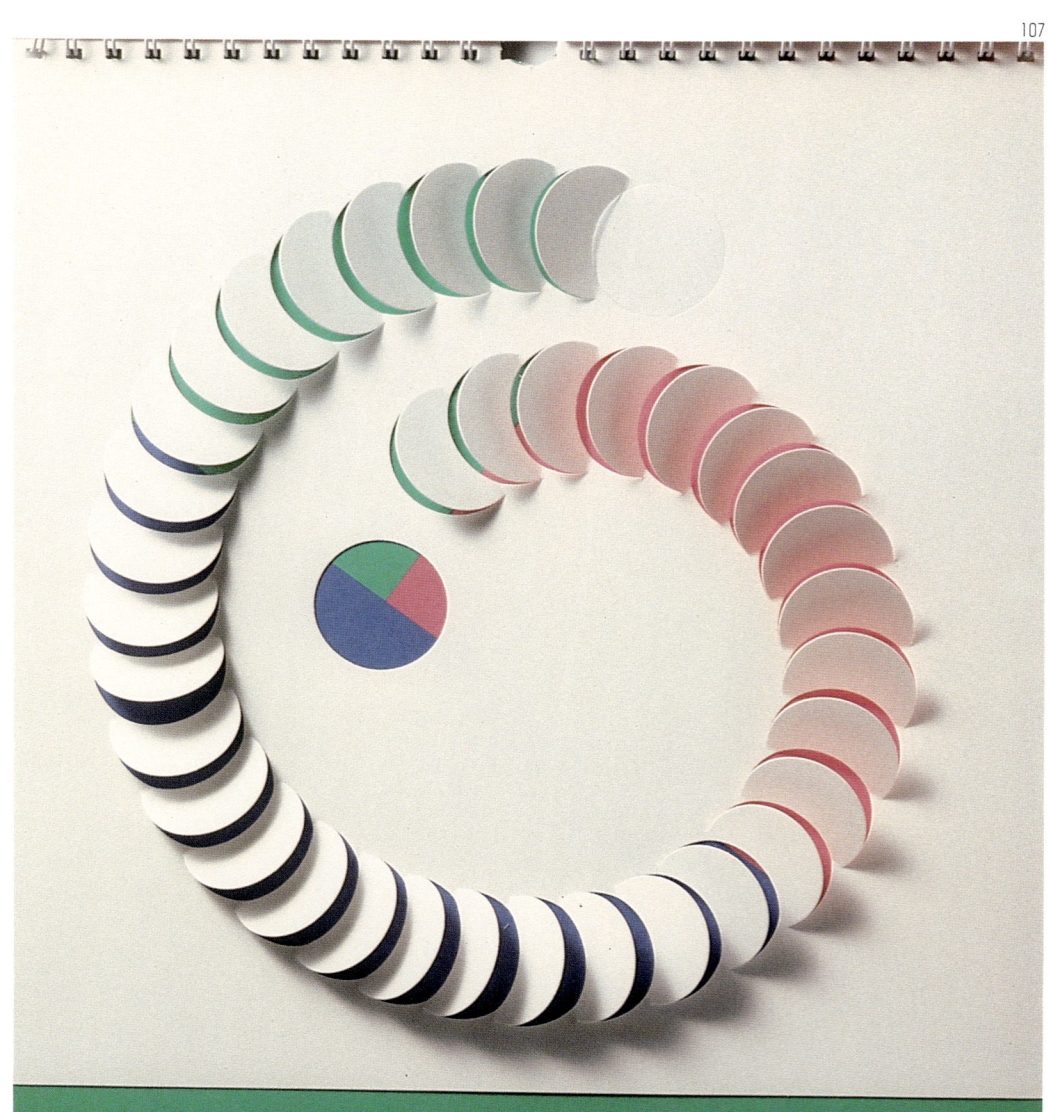

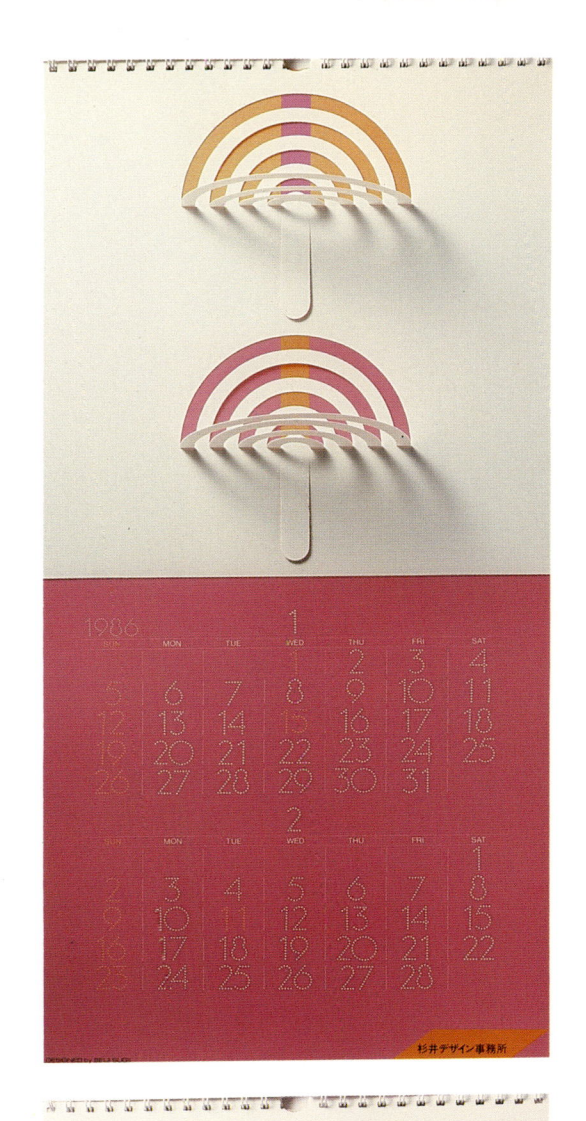

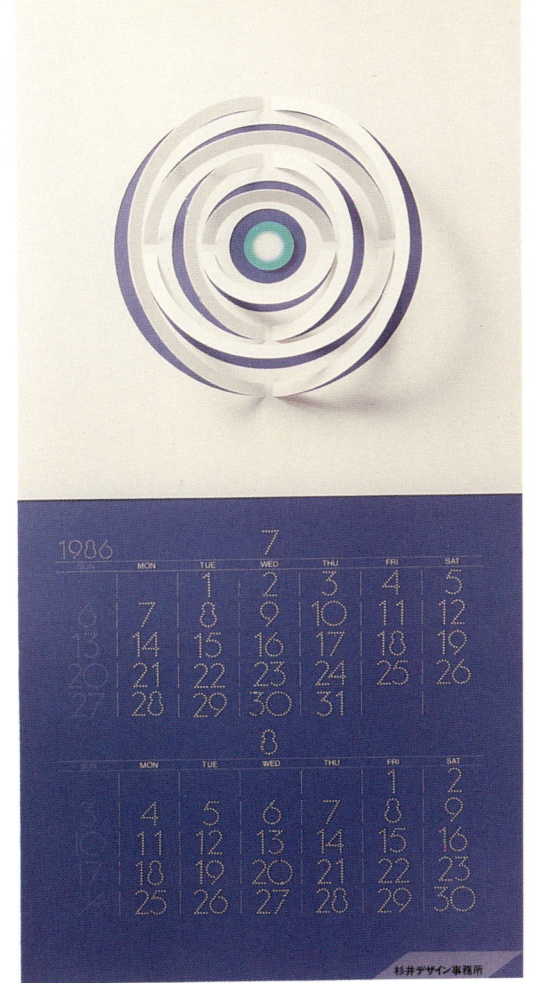

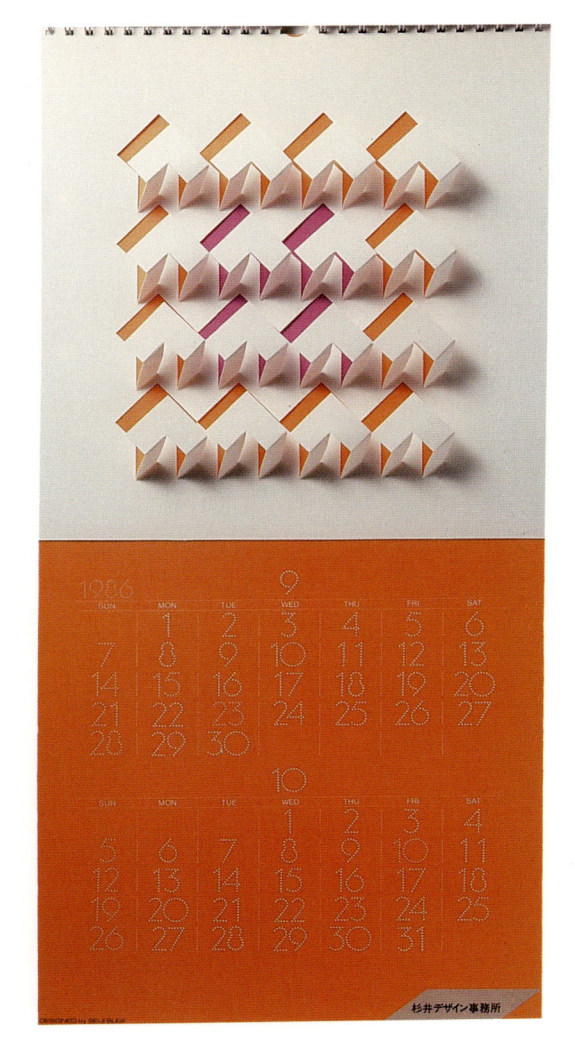

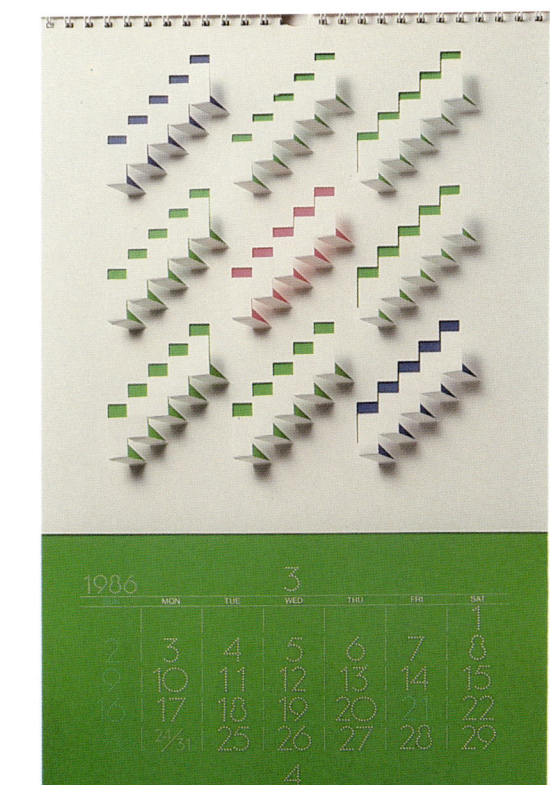

108
ハーモニー、1984
AD 三木 健
DE 三木 健
MA 三木 健
CL イディヨーロッパ
(イタリア)
中央の透けてみえる折り重なった模様が、1枚ずつめくるたびに変化するカレンダー

108

Calendar, 1984
AD Ken Miki
DE Ken Miki
MA Ken Miki
CL EDI Europa Sal, Milano
The see-through, layered part in the center changes its shape and color as each leaf is turned over.

Luglio/July/Juillet/Juli															1984
1	2	3	4	5	6	7	8	9	10	11	12	13	14	15	16
17	18	19	20	21	22	23	24	25	26	27	28	29	30	31	

Agosto/August/Août/August															
1	2	3	4	5	6	7	8	9	10	11	12	13	14	15	16
17	18	19	20	21	22	23	24	25	26	27	28	29	30	31	

© IDK design **HARMONY** Ken Miki

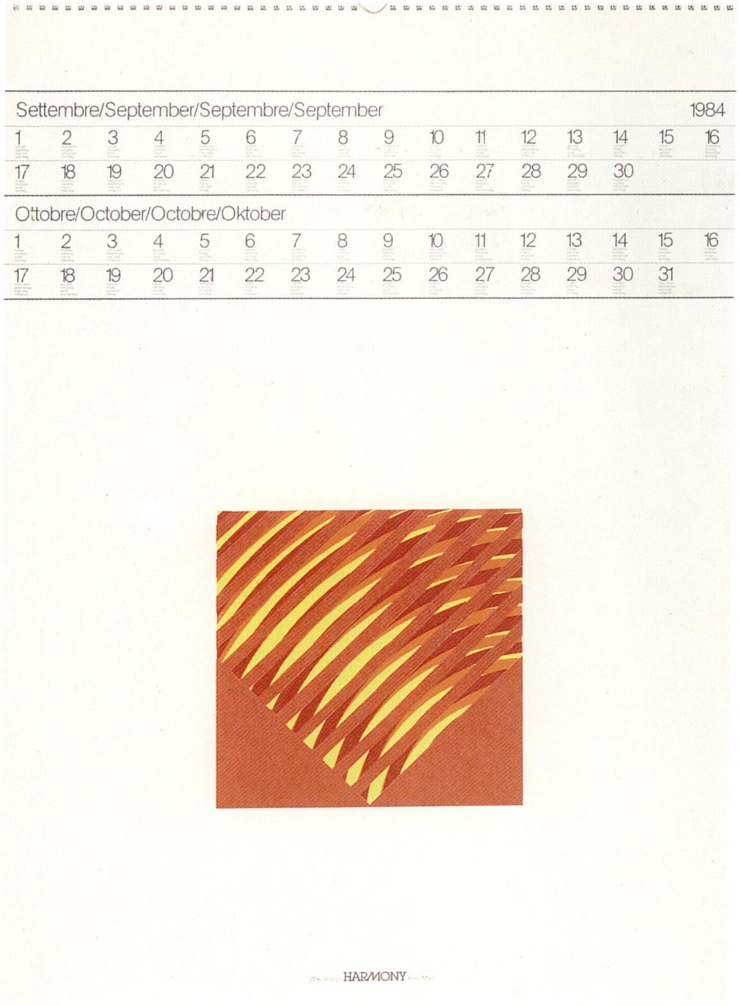

Settembre/September/Septembre/September															1984
1	2	3	4	5	6	7	8	9	10	11	12	13	14	15	16
17	18	19	20	21	22	23	24	25	26	27	28	29	30		

Ottobre/October/Octobre/Oktober															
1	2	3	4	5	6	7	8	9	10	11	12	13	14	15	16
17	18	19	20	21	22	23	24	25	26	27	28	29	30	31	

HARMONY

Gennaio/January/Janvier/Januar															1984
1	2	3	4	5	6	7	8	9	10	11	12	13	14	15	16
17	18	19	20	21	22	23	24	25	26	27	28	29	30	31	

Febbraio/February/Fevrier/Februar															
1	2	3	4	5	6	7	8	9	10	11	12	13	14	15	16
17	18	19	20	21	22	23	24	25	26	27	28	29			

HARMONY

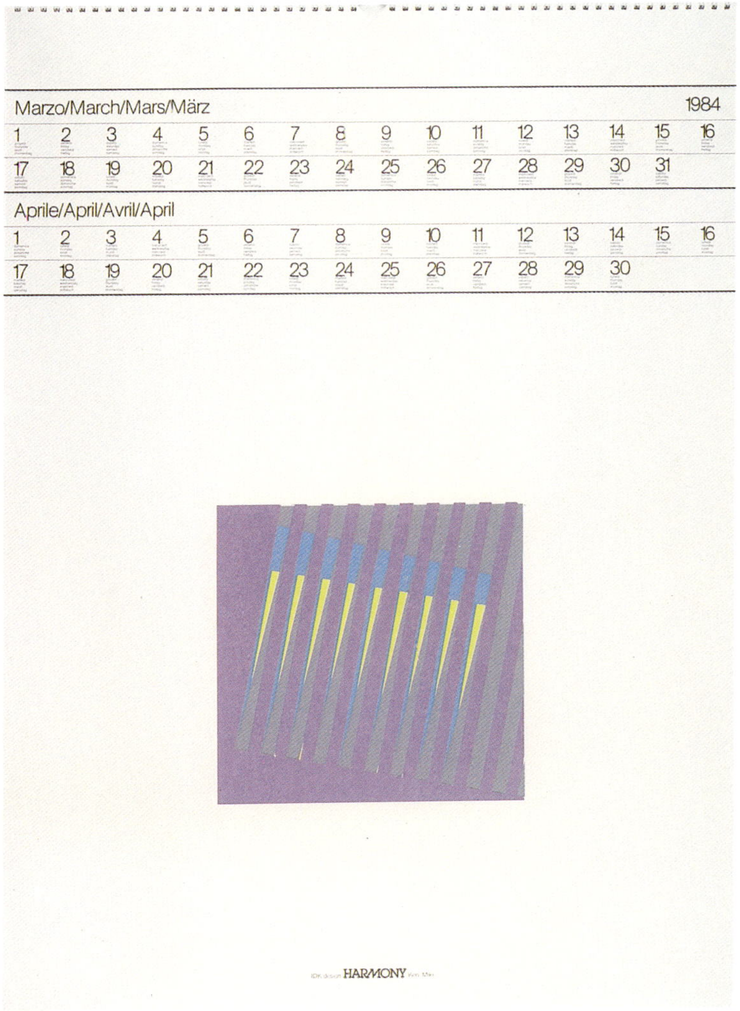

Marzo/March/Mars/März															1984
1	2	3	4	5	6	7	8	9	10	11	12	13	14	15	16
17	18	19	20	21	22	23	24	25	26	27	28	29	30	31	

Aprile/April/Avril/April															
1	2	3	4	5	6	7	8	9	10	11	12	13	14	15	16
17	18	19	20	21	22	23	24	25	26	27	28	29	30		

HARMONY

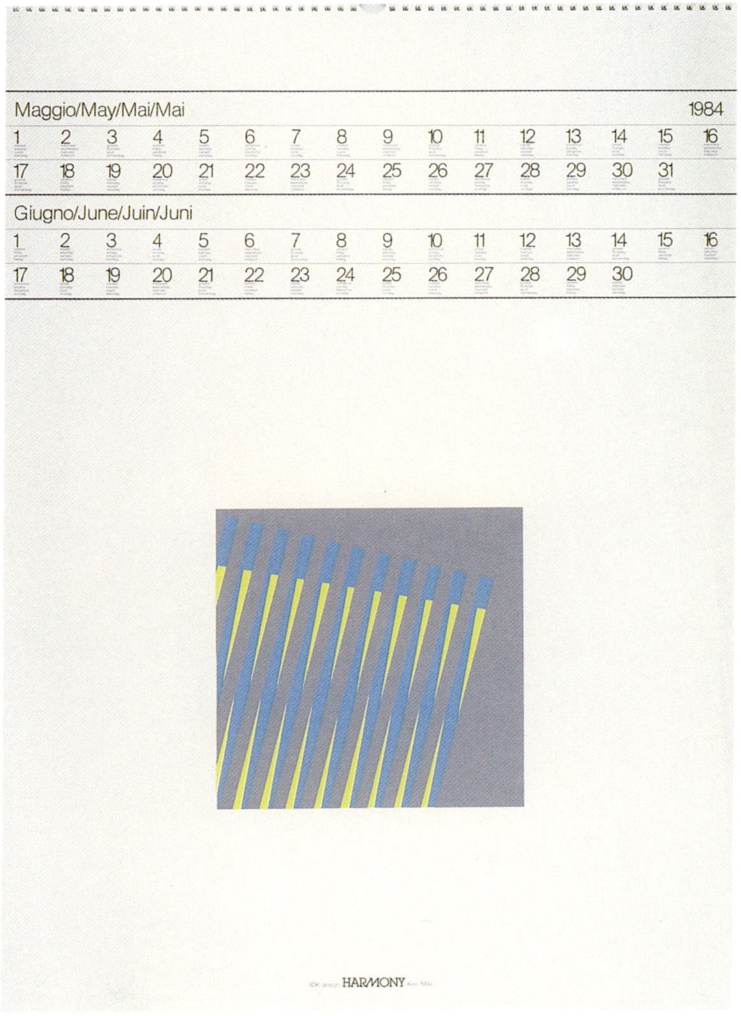 Maggio/May/Mai/Mai															1984
1	2	3	4	5	6	7	8	9	10	11	12	13	14	15	16
17	18	19	20	21	22	23	24	25	26	27	28	29	30	31	

Giugno/June/Juin/Juni															
1	2	3	4	5	6	7	8	9	10	11	12	13	14	15	16
17	18	19	20	21	22	23	24	25	26	27	28	29	30		

HARMONY

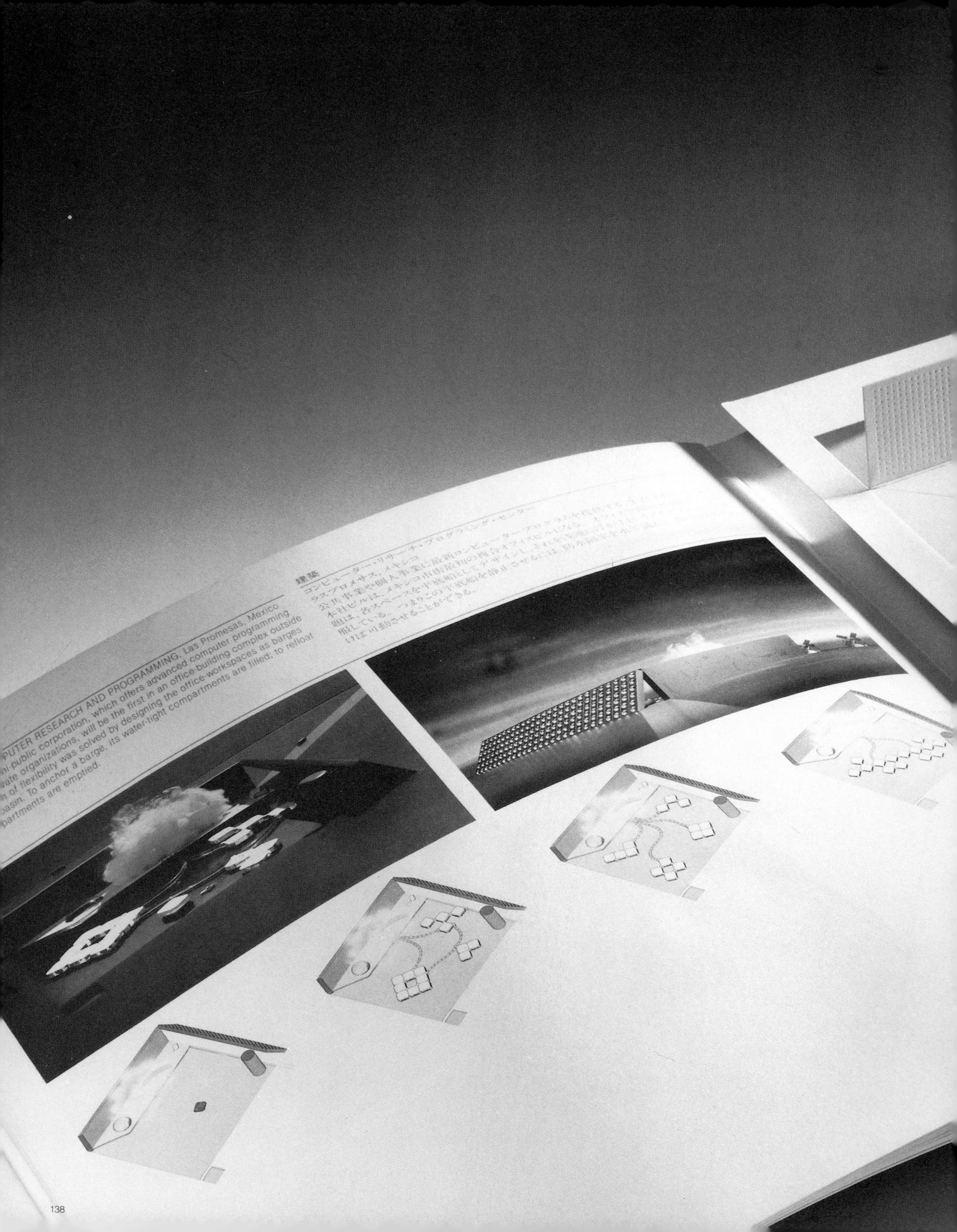

PUTER RESEARCH AND PROGRAMMING, Las Promesas, Mexico
n public corporation, which offers advanced computer programming
ate organizations, will be the first in an office-building complex programming
n of flexibility was solved by designing the office-workspaces as barges
asin. To anchor a barge, its water-tight compartments are filled; to refloat
partments are emptied.

建築
コンピューターリサーチ・プログラミング・センター
ラス・プロメサス、メキシコ
公共事業や個人事業に最新のコンピュータープログラムを提供する
本社ビルは、メキシコ市市街地初の複合オフィスビルになる。オフィス
間は、各スペースを平底船舶としてデザインし、それぞれ独立してう
せている。つまりこの平底船舶を移動させるには、防水隔室を水で満
けば可動させることができる。

109

アンバース展カタログ、1985
AD　エミリオ・アンバース
DE　エミリオ・アンバース
MA　大日本印刷
CL　アクシス

109

Catalogue, 1985
AD　Emilio Ambasz
DE　Emilio Ambasz
MA　Dai Nippon Printing
CL　Axis

Get better than ever storewide business
DEL MONTE ROUND
NOW... CASH IN
ON THE EXCITING
FLAVOR OF THE WEST!
Fill your saddle bags with silver!
DEL MONTE ROUND-UP
SEPT. 26
to NOV. 2
Del Monte FOODS
The bonanza trail
leads right through
your store. Just turn
page and stand back!

110

デルモンテ雑誌折込広告、1964
DE インタービジュアルコミ
　　ュニケーションズ(USA)
CL デルモンテ

110

Magazine Insert, 1964
DE Intervisual Communica-
　　tions, California
CL Del Monte

540 · Powell Street

- The most important building
- The "HEADQUARTER"
- It needs a New sign!

540 · Powell Street

- "Did you recognize the big computer-controlled 'Display Screen' at the Olympics?"
- The New sign has likeness.

625 · Sutter Street

- The awnings are removed.
- The beautyness is recovered.
- An open Galleria enhances now the function of the building.
- Marble, Steel and Neon.

625 · Sutter Street

- The Sign is a calendar,
- it is an electronic easel,
- it is in MOTION as WE are.

111

ポップアップブック、1985
DE　ダニエル・ロリ
MA　ダニエル・ロリ
美術学校の未来のイメージを、平面及びPop-upのイラストレーションで表現。折りあわせの頁がそれぞれ同一建物になっている。

111

Pop-up Book
"The future image", 1985
DE　Daniel Lori
MA　Daniel Lori
The future image of an art school is expressed by plane and pop-up illustrations on counter pages.

112

113
114

112・113・114
タカラポップアップ・ディスプレイ、
1987
AD 上田雄二
DE 丹司典孝
IL 七條成子
PH 篠原幸男
CL 宝酒造
1987年5月から翌年3月までの10回シリーズのうちの3点。立体イラストレーションを使ったP.O.P.広告

112・113・114
Pop-up Display, 1987
AD Yuji Ueda
DE Noritaka Tanji
IL Nariko Shichijo
PH Yukio Shinohara
CL Takara Shuzo
Three out of 10 in a series displayed from May, 1987 to March 1988. A point of purchase advertisement using three-dimensional graphics

115a
115b

146

115a・b
事務所10周年記念トランプ、1987
AD 勝岡重夫
DE 勝岡重夫
   勝岡重夫デザイン室
パッケージ
AD 勝岡重夫、松井桂三
DE 松井桂三
AG 松井桂三デザイン室
CL 勝岡重夫デザイン室
勝岡重夫デザイン室の10周年を記念して、10年間に制作されたシンボルマークをトランプに仕立てた。

115a・b
Playing Cards to Commemorate the 10th Anniversary of a Design Office, 1987
AD Shigeo Katsuoka
DE Shigeo Katsuoka
   Shigeo Katsuoka Design Studio
Packaging
AD Shigeo Katsuoka
   Keizo Matsui
DE Keizo Matsui
AG Keizo Matsui and Associates
CL Shigeo Katsuoka Design Studio
The symbol marks designed by Shigeo Katsuoka Design Studio in the past decade are tailored for playing cards. Mementoes for the 10th anniversary.

116・117
LOVE/HEART, 1982
AD 三木 健
DE 三木 健
MA 三木 健
CL フランス屋製菓
バレンタインデー用パッケージ

116・117
Packaging, 1982
AD Ken Miki
DE Ken Miki
MA Ken Miki
CL Furansuya
Packaging for St.Valentine's Day products

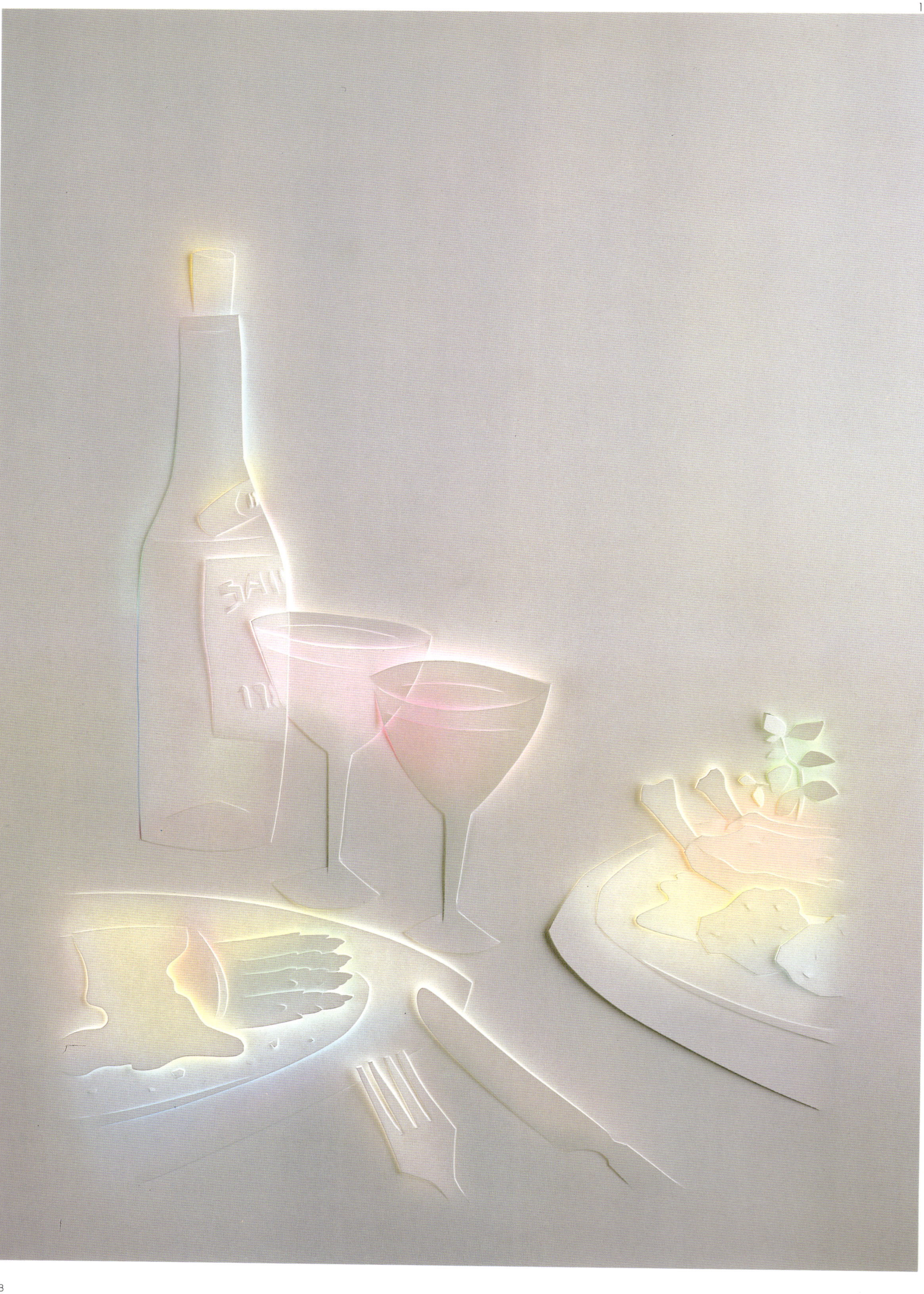

118~123
Slit Work
DE 駒井嘉樹
MA 駒井嘉樹
PH 駒井嘉樹
CL No.121, No.123-日本楽器製造
　　No.118-石亭
制作年 No.120, No.122-1983
　　　No.121, No.123-1986
　　　No.118, No.119-1987
1枚の紙を切る、折るなどして制作。No.119は、色の異なった別々の紙をはめ込み、1枚の紙にしてから制作された。

118~123
Slit Work Illustration
DE Yoshiki Komai
MA Yoshiki Komai
PH Yoshiki Komai
CL No.121, No.123-Nippon Gakki
　　No.118-Sekitei
Completion No.120, No.122-1983
　　　　　No.121, No.123-1986
　　　　　No.118, No.119-1987
Illustration by cutting and folding a piece of paper. Pieces of different colored paper are inlaid to make No.119.

TURNS UP WITH A CROWD OF BOY

THE SAME THREADS RE

LIKES TO DRESS UP IN

EVERY LITTLE

STEAL EVERYONE'S BOY FRIE

CAN GET

NO WHITE WINE, NO CREAM

120
121

150

122
123

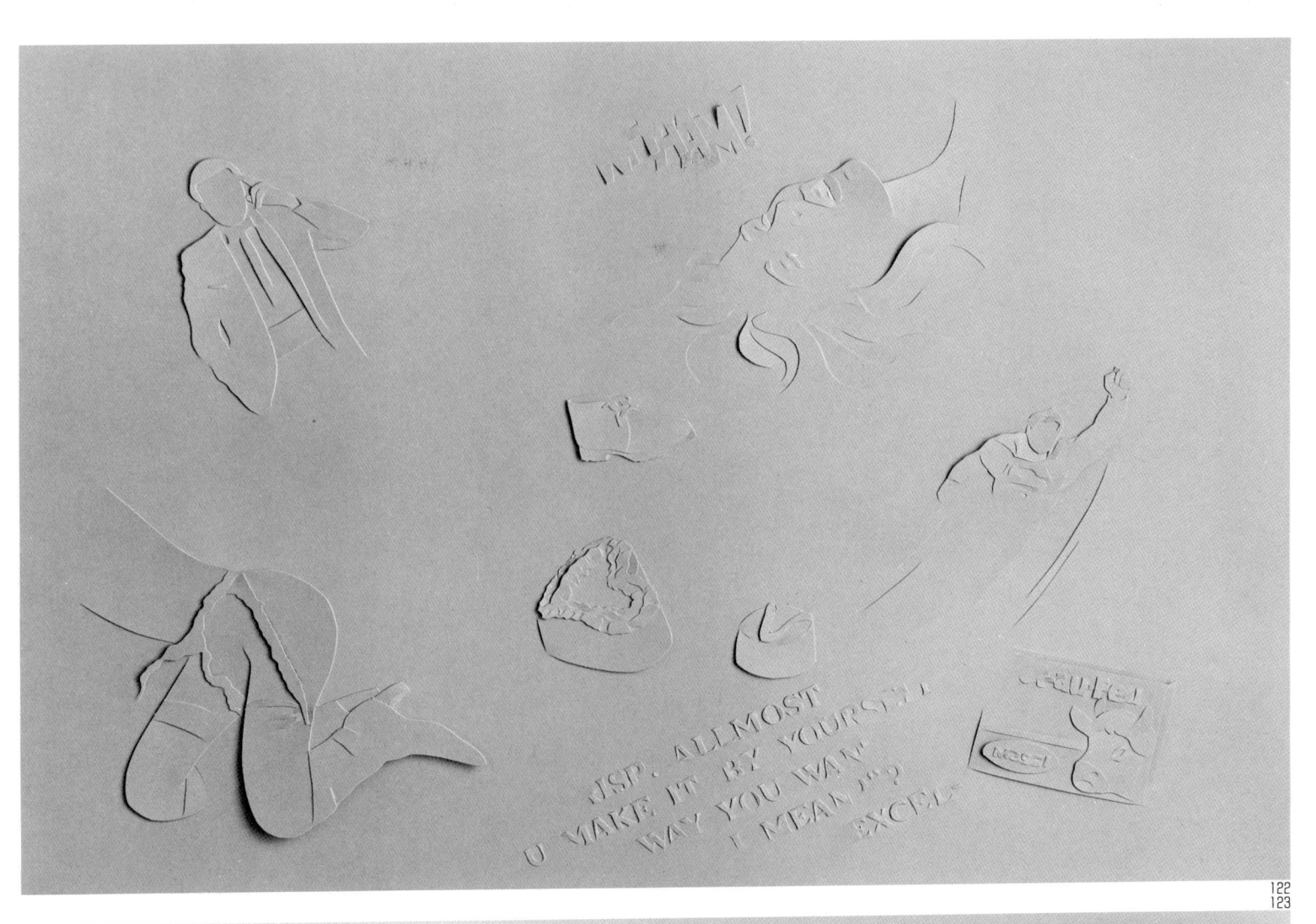

151

154
**THREE-DIMENSIONAL GREETING CARDS
AND DIRECT MAILS IN THE UNITED STATES**
Shin'ichiro Tora

アメリカにおける3DのカードとDM
虎 新一郎

158
PROFILE

作家プロフィール

アメリカにおける3DのカードとDM
虎 新一郎

日本とアメリカにおける各種行事での大きな習慣の違いは、アメリカでは、グリーティングカードの使用が日本と比較して格段に多く、またカードが各種行事の重要な役割を果たしていることである。

日本では中元・歳暮や誕生祝いなど贈答品の方に重点が置かれており、グリーティングカードの使用はやっと最近になって若い人達の間で行われるようになってきたが、やはり旧来のしきたりが強く、なかなかカードをおくるという習慣が定着しにくいようだ。他方、アメリカでは、どんな町の文具店・ブックストアー・ギフトショップなどでも、ありとあらゆる種類の行事にあわせたグリーティングカードが取揃えられており、不意の招待や返礼に、カードが直ちに間に合うようになっていて大変便利である。

アメリカには最大の年中行事であるクリスマスをトップにして、7つの大きな公式の祝祭日がある。人種の坩堝といわれるニューヨークでは、各国人種別の祭日・習慣・行事や宗教別など千差万別のグリーティングカードが販売されており、グリーティングカードなしでは、アメリカのすべての行事は存在しないといってよい程である。誕生から墓場までの人生の縮図が、すべてグリーティングカードで代行されているということだろう。

個人的な行事は勿論のこと、会社内での送別・歓迎パーティ、誕生祝いから婚約・結婚・出産・告別とすべてカードが主体となっている。超大形から変形・3D・ユーモア・ポップアートと、その行事を最高に盛り上げるカードが最上の贈り物となる。カードによってコミュニケーションが生まれるというわけである。また、カードをおくる側としても、個性的なカードを選んで印象づけ、器用な人は手作りのカードを制作する。そして特別に印象深い貴重なカードは、記念として保存する人達が多い。

手作りによるカードは、特別に自分のために制作されたという優越感や個人的な欲望を満足させるだけでなく、他に同種のものがないというアート的な唯一性を与えるからで、印刷された市販のカードよりも、手作り・手書きによるカードのもつ個性的なクラフト性が珍重されるのである。日本でもデザイナー間で交換する年賀状は、たとえ印刷されたものであっても個性的なクリエイティビティが表現されているので、これも一種の手作りカードといえるだろう。

アメリカの昨今の傾向として、アートブームがあげられるが、これは一般の人々の間に物に対する価値観や購買感覚に変化が起こってきたからなのである。精神的にも感覚的にも、表現がより自由となってきたアメリカの社会環境の変化によるものといえる。いつの時代にも必要性よりも満足感をもとめる人達がいるが、かつては一部の人々にもたれたこの感覚が、一般の人々に拡大・拡散され、伝達されてきたものと思われる。

この傾向の流れの大きな特徴として、人々の間に影響を与えるものにアートがあり、こうして人々はかつての統一化されたデザイン・ブランドよりも、個性的なアート・ブランドをもとめ、グッドデザインよりもクラフト・アートを望むようになってきた。これらの影響を素早く受けた若い人達は、外面的な視覚の影響よりも、内面的な価値観やセンスといった心理的かつ理知的な要素をより重要視している。

このアートブームはグリーティングカードの世界にも影響し、芸術的なセンスとしてのニューウェイブアートやポップアートのカードが、これまでの行事的なカードよりも好まれ、知的な雰囲気をもつレトロ調のもの等、芸術思考的なグリーティングカードに人気が集まっている。また、不特定な行事にも使用出来るアート表紙のみのカードも出現し、自分好みの絵入りメッセージも書くことが出来るので、若い人達の間で好評を博している。

変化するカード、いわゆる3Dカードもこれ等のアート好きの若者達に人気があり、ポップアップ式やスライドさせることによって絵の変わる漫画チックなもの、レトロ調としての古い映画名作ポスターを立体化させたものが好まれている。ただ、種類も少なく、単価も他のカードに

比べて高いため、やや購売力が落ちるようである。しかしこうした若い人達は、これまでの人々と違って、同じ絵柄のものを選ばず、クリスマスカードさえも多量に幾種もの変化を求めて購入する傾向がある。そのためアーティスト達の手になる個性的なグリーティングカードは、少量生産・販売に移行してきた。これは各種行事のカードにおいても、適切な販売方法ともいえるだろう。特にミュージアム・ストアーなど特殊な売店でのアートカードの売り上げが増加しているのは、勿論アートブームの影響が強いためといえる。

こうしてニューヨークの人々は、特にアート的なインテリアで部屋を飾り、アート感覚のファッションを身につけて個性的な生活を楽しんでいるわけだが、こうした生活を楽しむというアート感覚が拡大されることによって、企業のDMコンセプトにも影響を及ぼしてきている。

DMとは、そもそも企業としての無店舗販売、マーケットをセグメントすることによって適切な商品、またはサービス・情報を直接に顧客に提供することが主要なファクターとなっている。この個人的なアプローチという直接的メッセージの伝達に、アート的なインフォメーションによるコミュニケートが行われるようになってきた。このアート感覚を伝達する手段としての、ポップアートやサイケデリックな画風のもの、クラフト的な立体、3Dによる商品や製品名を注目させ印象づける、立体アートデザインがある。

この立体アートは特殊なDMだけに、制作コストも高く、余程のプロフィットが高いものだけに使用され、特に郵送料の値上げもあって昨今の企業としては、予算削減のために3DのDM制作は少ない。むしろ企業としては、S.P.やP.O.P.といったカウンター・ディスプレイにこれらの予算が流れ、デザイン云々よりも消費者、店主のプロフィットを重要視しているようである。しかし、ファッション・化粧品といったアート的雰囲気を売りものとする企業では、DMとしてこの3Dが制作されている。

一方で特にパッケージング・デザインの有り方が、旧来の製品名だけを表記したものから、消費者への直接のアプローチの広告までをも兼用する程のものとなり、3DのDMを発送するよりも、サンプル・パッケージを直接、消費者に発送する、一石二鳥の効果的手段をとり始めたことも、立体DMの制作が減少した原因の一つかもしれない。しかし現代のアートとカルチャーの社会においては、すでに生活必需品が豊富に市場にあふれ、単なる機能や便利さをもとめたデザインより個性を重要視するアート的な社会となった。生み出されるアート的な作品によってお互いのコミュニケーションを起こさせ、企業にとってもアートを通じて消費者とのコミュニケーションをもつことが、最大の効果的な企業の成長につながるものといえるだろう。特に日本の伝統あるクラフト技術と、日本独特の遊び心を発揮した立体アートが、国際的なコミュニケーションの場を拡げることを大いに期待しているものである。

ニューヨーク・アートディレクターズクラブ理事1986-1988
TGDコミュニケーショングループ主宰

Three-Dimensional Greeting Cards and
Direct Mails in the United States
Shin'ichiro Tora

The greatest contrast between Japanese and American customs for celebrating holidays is the extensive use of greeting cards in the United States. Americans use far more greeting cards, and more often than do the Japanese. Cards play an important role in American life, while in Japan sending gifts is a more accepted thing to do. Sending greeting cards is gaining popularity with younger Japanese but the old tradition of sending gifts prevails among older generations.

There are seven major holidays in the United States, Christmas being the most widely and extravagantly celebrated. In New York, which has been called a melting pot of races, greeting cards in a variety of languages and marking a multitude of ethnic and religious holidays are sold. From birth to death, Americans mark both the major and minor events of life by sending each other greeting cards.

This tremendous variety of occasions for cards has led to a wide-ranging panorama of types and styles—large, small, odd shaped, 3-dimensional, pop-up, humorous, sentimental, solemn and joyful.

Many people pride themselves on their ability to choose the "perfect" card for a person or occasion. They spend hours making careful selections. Others take their time and trouble to create original, hand-made cards. Many of these can become collector's items. Beautiful if it was made just for him or her, but satisfies the desire of most people to have something unique. The art boom recently seen in America is partly engendered by an overall increase in consumption as well as social changes which have encouraged freer expression on both the spiritual and sensitivity levels. This in turn has had an clear influence on greeting cards. Cards employing new wave art, pop art, or more reflective art with an intelligent atmosphere have gained ground on the more conventional holiday illustrations. Cards with artistic cover but blank inside for the sender to create his or her own message have become popular with young people.

The so-called 3-dimensional cards, ones often called holography cards in which the picture appears to change as it is viewed from different angles, and pop-up art have become popular among the pop-art loving young set. In particular, cards which have comical pop-up art or create an effect by a sliding part as well as 3-dimensional cards made from posters of masterpieces of old favorite movies are very popular. Unfortunately, these unusual cards are still more expensive than the other ordinary ones.

Young people tend to seek these different, out-of-the-ordinary cards, and in response, card manufacturers have begun to produce small quantities of such special cards. Also, the sales of art cards at the shop of museums and galleries are increasing, and this, too, is certainly an outgrowth of the art boom.

This movement into unusual art on the part of card manufacturers is now influencing art concepts in the field of direct mails. Companies now seek to send a direct personal message through the use of specially designed artistic devices which they feel to characterize their company or product. The entire span of new types, 3-dimensional, pop-art based on psychedelic graphics, craftwork, are used to impress the firm's name or product name on the consumer.

These very special materials however, are used sparingly, due to the high cost of production. They are unusually reserved for projected high-return mailings or point-of-purchase displays. Increasing mailing costs also affect the decision to use these unusual items. They find the broadest use in high profit lines like fashion or cosmetics where an artistic mood can often increase sales on what are usually high-priced, high-markup items.

Special packaging seems to have become an additional communication tool these days and many firms seem to prefer sending samples to potential consumers.

However, in the present affluent and high-consumption society, art emphasizing individuality came to replace designs seeking for functionality and convenience. Art can serve as a most effective way for corporations to communicate with consumers and promote their own growth.

I hope that 3-dimensional art in the greeting card and direct mail field which are created with the traditional craftmanship and skill of Japan will become a broader channel for international communications.

Member, Board of Directors,
Art Directors Club, New York
Creative Director,
TGD Communication Group

PROFILE
作家プロフィール

Emilio Ambasz
アンバース，エミリオ

1943年アルゼンチン生まれ。アメリカのプリンストン大学および大学院卒業。ニューヨーク近代美術館キューレーター、プリンストン大学教授、ドイツのウルム造形大学客員教授などを歴任。現在、自分のデザイン・オフィスを主宰して、建築、ディスプレイ、インダストリアル、グラフィック、都市環境など各分野のデザインコンサルタント活動をしている。プログレッシブ・アーキテクチュア賞をはじめとする建築・インテリア関係の賞、さらにインダストリアル関係の賞も多数受賞している。個展も、世界各地で開催している。
主な作品は、スペイン・コルドバの個人住宅、テキサスのサン・アントニオ植物園、グランドラピッズコミュニティーアートセンター、ニューヨークのアメリカ民芸博物館、「バーティブラ・シーティング・システム」「ロゴテック・スポットライト」などがある。

Born in Argentine in 1943. M. Arch, Princeton University, U.S.A. Was a curator of design, the Museum of Modern Art, New York. Co-founder of the Institute for Architecture and Urban Studies in New York. Taught at Princeton University and Hochschüle für Gestaltung in Ulm, Germany as a visiting professor and others. Presently, president of Emilio Ambasz & Associates Inc., and involved in architecture, industrial, urban environmental, graphic, exhibit designs and design consultancy.
Won numerous prizes and honors including Progressive Architecture Prize, SMAU Prize, Compasso d'Ore Prize. Held numerous one-man shows in the United States, Europe and Japan.
His major works include: The Museum of American Folk Art, San Antonio Botanical Conservatory, Community Arts Center (Grand Rapids), Bruxelles Lambert Bank, Mercedes-Benz Showroom, "Vertebra" seating system, and others.

Emilio Ambasz & Associates Inc.
632 Broadway,
New York, NY 10012,
U.S.A.
phone: 212-420-8850

Akio Okumura
奥村昭夫

1943年生まれ。ハウス食品工業・サントリー・牛乳石鹸共進社・松下電器産業等のパッケージデザイン及び、火遊びはいつもおもしろい展・パッケージングクリエイト中国西安展・ポスト展・おおさかの人展・表彰状展・蔡小楓展等のプロデュースを行う。

㈱パッケージングクリエイト
〒530 大阪市北区西天満
5-13-11 大東ビル2F
phone 06-312-7978

Born in 1943.
Major Design Works:
Packages for House Food Industrial, Suntory, Cow Brand Soap Kyoshinsha, Matsushita Electric Industrial, etc.
Producing Work: "Playing with fire is always interesting" Exhibition, "Packaging Create-Xi'an, China" Exhibition, "Post" Exhibition, "People of Osaka, certificates of commendation" Exhibition, "Cai Xiao Feng" Exhibition

Packaging Create Inc.
Daito Building
5-13-11, Nishi Tenma,
Kita-ku, Osaka 530,
Japan
phone: 06-312-7978

Hiroyasu Kakimoto
柿本博康

1950年大阪生まれ。69年大阪市立工芸高等学校図案科卒業。同年Yarakasukan入社。その後、NIA、F-Brain、TCDに勤務、その間P.O.P.、販促、商品企画、グラフィック、パッケージ、C.I.等を手がける。85年 Kids Design Officeを設立。仕事内容は店舗、建築サイン・シンボル制作、C.I.、パッケージ、ポスター、グラフィック等、ジャンルにこだわらない。"生活とデザイン"がテーマで、人間の生活にかかわるものすべてがデザインだと思っている。今後、機会があればTOYや絵本等、純粋グラフィックの分野をやってみたい。

キッズデザインオフィス
〒530 大阪市北区茶屋町
6-18 パルベック404
phone 06-375-4758

Born in Osaka in 1950. Finished Osaka Municipal Art & Craft High School and employed by Yarakasukan in 1969.
Worked for NIA, F-Brain, TCD design offices, making P.O.P. advertisements, sales promotion tools, graphics, packages and corporate identities and merchandising.
In 1985, Established Kids Design Office.
The activity covers shops, signs & symbols, C.I.s, packages, posters, graphics, etc.
With "Life and Design" as a theme, every thing surrounding the life of a man is related with design. In the future, he hopes to be involved in toys, picture books and other purely graphic design.

Kids Design Office
No. 404, 6-18,
Chayamachi, Kita-ku,
Osaka 530, Japan
phone: 06-375-4758

Mitsuo Katsui
勝井三雄

1931年東京生まれ。56年東京教育大学芸術学科構成科卒業後、味の素入社。61年フリーランスとなり、勝井デザイン研究室主宰。65年毎日産業デザイン賞受賞、72年第3回講談社出版文化賞、ブルノブックデザインビエンナーレ(チェコスロバキア)金賞、東京ADC会員賞受賞、84年第11回ブルノグラフィックアートビエンナーレ招待講師及び審査員、伝統と現代技術・日本のグラフィックデザイナー12人展(フランス)、85年世界で最も美しい本展(東ドイツ)銅賞受賞。科学万博「講談社ブレインハウス」アートディレクター、ICOGRADA招待講師及び審査員。86年国際花と緑の博覧会シンボルマーク、87年第7回ラハティポスタービエンナーレ(フィンランド)受賞。現在、筑波大学非常勤講師。東京アートディレクターズクラブ委員。民族学博物館展示企画委員。日本グラフィックデザイナー協会理事。ビデオテックスクリエイターズ協会代表。日本文化デザイン会議メンバー。

勝井三雄デザイン研究室
〒107 東京都港区南青山
5-1-10-907
phone 03-407-0801

Born in Tokyo in 1931. 1956 — Graduated from Tokyo University of Education and employed by Ajinomoto. 1961 — Became free lance designer and established Mitsuo Katsui Institute of Design. Presently, Part-time lecturer, Tsukuba University.
Awards & Honors:
1965 — Mainichi Industrial Design Prize, 1972 — The 3rd Kodansha Publications Cultural Prize in Book Design Section, International Biennale of Graphic Design, Bruno (Gold Prize), Tokyo ADC Members' Prize, 1984 — Lecture/jury member, International Biennale of Graphic Design, Bruno, 1985 — "The Most Beautiful Book in the World Exhibition", East Germany (Bronze Prize), 1987 — Award, Lahti Poster Biennale, Finland
Major Involvement:
1985 — Art Director, Tsukuba Expo '85 Kodansha "Brain House", 1986 — Symbol Mark for the International Garden and Greenery Exposition
Membership:
Tokyo Art Directors Club Committee, National Ethnic Museum Exhibit Planning Committee, Japan Graphic Desingers Association, Videotex Creators Association, Japan Inter-Design Conference.

Mitsuo Katsui Institute of Design
No. 907, 5-1-10,
Minami Aoyama,
Minato-ku, Tokyo 107,
Japan
phone: 03-407-0801

Joyce Culkin
カルキン，ジョイス

ニューヨーク及びシカゴで10年間、フリーのアーチスト及びデザイナーとして働く。その後、平面を越えた媒体で、プロモーション用のコミュニケーションをはかることに興味をおぼえ、ペーパー・エンジニアリングの研究を始める。
現在、クライアントの斬新な販促用コンセプトづくりを手伝っている。案内状、招待状、パンフレット、パッケージ、P.O.P.展示用品などの他に、紙による製品模型もつくる。三次元のプロモーション作品の目指すところは、見る人に驚きを与え、コミュニケーション・プロセスに引き込むことである。
ボストンADC、AIGAニューヨーク、タイプディレクターズクラブニューヨークなどの各賞を受賞。『プリントマガジン』『コミュニケーンアーツ』(アメリカ)などに掲載される。

Worked for ten years as an independent artist/designer in New York City and Chicago. After working with two-dimensional visual format for years, developed an extensive understanding of paper engineering in the past ten years. She offers to clients an innovative way of presenting promotional concepts. This can take the form of invitations announcements, brochures, specialty packaging, P.O.P. display etc. Basically, she is selling creative ways for clients to present themselves or their product to the marketplace. The goal of the promotional piece is to surprise the viewer and make him a participant in the communication process. The pieces consistently generate interest and excitement. She also uses this language in paper for model making for product ideas that are translated into other materials.
Awards and publications: Boston Art Directors Club, AIGA New York, Type Directors Club New York, *Print Magazine*, *CA*, *Simpson Paper Company*, *Champion Paper*

Dimensional Design
1514 Beacon Street
Brookline, MA 02146,
U.S.A.
phone: 617-731-9544

Yoshiki Komai
駒井嘉樹

1952年生まれ。75年京都教育大学特修美術科卒業。77年パーソンズスクールオブデザイン(ニューヨーク)で学ぶ。81年The New School of Social Researchメディア科大学院修士課程終了。83年Slit Work展(銀座・青画廊)。現在東京にて制作活動を続ける。Slit Workは、ニューヨークでファッション・フォトグラファーの仕事の中から生まれた。スタジオ撮影用のロールペーパーに、様々な細工を施し、ライトとの効果でモデルをより美しく撮るというペーパーワークが、帰国後それ自体作品として自立する。作品は常に1枚の紙から出来ている。情報化の進む現代社会をこのようなシンプルな方法で表現していきたい。

〒164 東京都中野区中野
5-45-11 紅葉ハイム203
phone 03-385-8954

Born in 1952.
1975 — Graduated from Kyoto University of Education. 1977 — Studied at Parsons School of Design. 1981 — Graduated from the post-graduate course, The New School of Social Research. 1983 — Slit Work Exhibition, Tokyo. Presently continues his creation activity in Tokyo.
Slit work was born out of fashion photographers in New York. Some devices are applied to the roll paper used for studio photography so that the model can be photographed more impressively by light effect. This method has become independent after his return to Tokyo, as his speciality paper work. Every piece of work is made of a sheet of paper. He wants to express present-day society with increasing information complication in a simple method like this.

No. 203 Momiji Heim,
5-45-11, Nakano,
Nakano-ku, Tokyo 164,
Japan
phone: 03-385-8954

Seiji Sugii
杉井清二

1935年生まれ。杉井デザイン事務所主宰。77年全米ADC「日本グラフィックアイデア'77」銀賞、78年全国カレンダー展大蔵省印刷局長賞、80年日本パッケージデザインニューヨーク展金賞、82年日本パッケージデザイン協会展テーマ賞、85年日本パッケージデザイン賞奨励賞受賞。71〜79年ペーパークリエイティブ展（銀座・松屋）5回、79、81、83、85年デザインフォーラム展出品。81〜86年個展チクタク展5回、84年松坂屋「愛の鐘」モニュメントクロック、86年墨田区中小企業センター大モニュメントクロック（東京）SDA賞。日本グラフィックデザイナー協会会員、日本パッケージデザイン協会会員。

Born in 1935. President of Sugii Design Office. Awards: 1977—Silver Medal, "Japan Graphic Idea '77", U.S.A. Art Director's Club, 1978—Director of Printing Bureau, Ministry of Finance Prize, National Calendar Exhibition, 1980—Gold Medal, Japan Package Design New York Exhibition, 1982—Award, Japan Package Design Association, 1985—Japan Package Design Award for Encouragement, 1986—SDA Prize Exhibitions: 1971〜79—Paper Creative Exhibition, Tokyo (5 times), 1979, 81, 83, 85—Design Forum Exhibition, 1981〜86—One-man Exhibition "Tick Tuck" (5 times), 1984—"Bell of Love" Monument Clock, Matsuzakaya Membership: Japan Graphic Designers Association, Japan Package Design Association

杉井デザイン事務所
〒457 名古屋市南区内田橋2-11-8
phone 052-691-9529

Sugii Design Office
2-11-8, Uchidabashi,
Minami-ku, Nagoya 457,
Japan
phone: 052-691-9529

Koji Tashiro
田代耕司

1941年岩手県宮古市生まれ。64年岩手大学特設美術科構成科卒業後、岡山県笠岡市立新吉中学校教諭を勤める。66年岩手大学教育学部専攻科、67年東北紙工企画デザイン室勤務、68年学習研究社入社、主として、小学校入学前の子どもたちを対象とした絵本・教材類の企画開発を担当、現在に至る。ANIMAL BOX（小さな箱を開いていくと、数メートルのヘビになるなど）、ORIMALS（長い1枚の紙を折り込んでいくと、いろいろな動物の形になる）、ANIMAL'S HEART（ハートの形が組み込まれた動物のモビール）、立体的に展開するクリスマスカードなど紙を主体とした作品を制作。『とびだすカード』（ポプラ社）、『作って楽しむペーパークラフト』（共著、文化出版局）出版。

Born in 1941 in Iwate, 1964—Graduated from Iwate University and taught art in a junior high school. 1967—Worked for Planning and Design Unit of a paper engineering company. 1968—Employed by Gakken, engaged mainly in developing picture books and instructive materials for pre-school children Major Dimensional Works: ANIMAL BOX—When a small box is opened, it turns to a several-meter-long snake. ORIMALS—When a long piece of paper is folded, it turns to different animals. ANIMAL'S HEART —Mobiles of animal with the shape of heart incorporated. Three-dimensional Christmas cards, New Year's cards.
Publications: *Popping-up Cards, Enjoy making paper craft* (Joint Work)

学習研究社
幼児局デザイン室
〒107 東京都港区南青山2-2-15 ウィン青山ビル221
phone 03-404-8411

Child Design Office
Gakken
No. 221, 2-2-15,
Minami Aoyama,
Minato-ku, Tokyo 107,
Japan
phone: 03-404-8411

Tsuneo Taniuchi
谷内庸生

1953年和歌山県生まれ。75年日本大学芸術学部卒業。デザイン会社勤務後、78年渡米。79〜82年ボストンの教育テレビ局WGBH、W.F.E.M建築事務所に勤務。82年ボストンにスタジオ設立。ニューヨーク近代美術館、ボストン美術館、ハーバード大学などをクライアントとして、編集デザイン、ポスター、ロゴタイプ、カードデザインなどのデザイン活動を続ける。80年タイプディレクターズクラブ銅賞、82・83年ニューイングランド・ブックショーのデザイン賞、83年ボストンADC銅賞、ニューヨークADC編集部門賞受賞。85年草月会館にて個展。83年『アルファベット・ランデブー』自費出版、85年『かみ彫刻』（玄光社刊）、87年『かみ彫刻2』（同社刊）出版。

Born in Wakayama in 1953. 1975—Graduated from Nihon University, College of Art. 1979〜82—Worked for WGBH, Boston Educational TV Foundation, and W.F.E.M. Architect Office. 1982—Established Taniuchi Design Studio in Boston. Awards: 1980—Bronze Medal, Type Directors Club Awards for Typographic Excellence, 1982, 83—Design Prize, New England Book Show, 1983 — Boston and New York ADC Award, for Editorial Design.
Exhibition: 1985—One-man show, Tokyo.
Publication: *Alphabet Rendevous* (self-promotion), 1983, *Paper Sculpture* (Genko-sha), 1985, *Paper Sculpture II*, (Genko-sha), 1987

36 Flint Street No. 3,
Sommerville, MA 02145,
U.S.A.
phone: 617-628-6534

Masahiro Chatani
茶谷正洋

1934年広島生まれ。56年東京工業大学卒業後、大成建設設計部入社。61〜69年建設省建築研究所、67年工学博士、69〜80年東京工業大学助教授、77年ワシントン大学客員助教授、80年東京工業大学教授となり、現在に至る。82年から折り紙建築の展覧会を国内・海外で開催。『折り紙建築』(彰国社)をはじめとして、『マジックハウス』(雄鶏社)、『とびだすおりがみ』(ポプラ社)、『異次元グリーティングカード』(雄鶏社)、『折り紙建築世界の建築めぐり』(彰国社)など著書は10数冊に及ぶ。

東京工業大学茶谷研究室
〒152 東京都目黒区大岡山 2-12-1
phone 03-726-1111

Born in Hiroshima in 1934. 1956—Graduated from Tokyo Institute of Technology, and employed by Taisei (design department). 1961 ~ 69—Building Research Institute, Ministry of Construction and received Doctor's Degree in Engineering in 1967. 1969 ~ 80—Assistant Professor, Tokyo Institute of Technology, 1977—Visiting Associate Professor, University of Washington, U.S.A. 1980—Professor, Tokyo Institute of Technology, 1982—Started ORIGAMIC Architecture (paper-folded architecture) shows at home and abroad. Publications: *Origamic Architecture, Popping out Paper-craft, Magic House, Greeting Cards of Other Dimensions, Buildings Around the World by ORIGAMIC Architecture* etc.

Chatani Research Office
Tokyo Institute of Technology
2-12-1, Ookayama,
Meguro-ku, Tokyo 152,
Japan
phone: 03-726-1111

Kenzo Nakagawa
中川憲造

1947年大阪生まれ。高島屋宣伝部を経て、73年ボルト・ナッツスタジオ設立。75年日本デザインセンター入社、現在同社総合グラフィックス研究室室長。デザインディレクターとして、伊勢丹のインフォメーションデザイン、トヨタ自動車の企業広告、世界野生生物基金の子供新聞PANDAの編集デザインなどを、延山博保、森上暁のスタッフらと制作。79年東京ADC賞、80年ブルノグラフィックビエンナーレ特別賞(チェコスロバキア)受賞。

㈱日本デザインセンター
〒104 東京都中央区銀座 1-13-13 中央大和ビル
phone 03-567-3231

Born in Osaka in 1947. Employed by Takashimaya Department Store in Osaka where he engaged in advertisement for 7 years. 1973—Established Bolt & Nuts Studio jointly with two other partners in Osaka. 1975 — Employed by Nippon Design Center, at present, Chief of Total Graphics Research Office of the Center. Involved in information design for Isetan Department Store, corporate advertisement for Toyota Motor, editorial design of PANDA, child's newspaper of World Wild Life Funds and others.
Awards: 1979—Tokyo ADC Award, 1980 — Special Prize, International Biennale of Graphic Design in Bruno

Nippon Design Center Inc.
Chuo Yamato Building
1-13-13, Ginza, Chuo-ku,
Tokyo 104, Japan
phone: 03-567-3231

Lyn Hourahine
フラーヒン, リン

イギリス、サウス・ウェルズ生まれ。大学在学中に全国スターパックス・パッケージング最高賞を受賞。企業のデザイン部勤務、デザイン・コンサルタントを経て、1979年、パッケージング・デザイン会社を設立。その後、紙を二次元、三次元に使ったカードその他のデザインを専門とするペーパー・パワーを分離独立させる。"デザインの新開地を拓くことを自分たちに課したんだ。ぼくたちのアプローチは、明るくって、創造性をかきたてるもので、自然の力を健全な実用性と結びつけ、しかも、ビジネスとしてやっていけるものを考えることなんだ。"

Born in South Wales (U.K.) and attended school and college in Newport, Gwent. At college, won the top accolade in the U.K.'s National Starpacks Packaging Award Competition for students, not only winning his category section but the overall Gold Prize for best entry.
In 1979 established Paper Power as a business activity to encapsulate and promote his three-dimensional skills in Paper Engineering design. Paper Power specializes in the innovative design of three-dimensional and flat-folding structures in paper, card and other related materials from pop-ups to sophisticated fold-outs, including postal presentations, packaging, promotional material, display, direct mail and three-dimensional effects for television.
"We have set ourselves the task of breaking new ground in this area of design. Our approach is positive, creatively inspiring, combining natural ability with sound commercial practicality, also having the resources and experience to design effectively within marketing and business criteria"

Paper Power
15A South Parade,
Bedford Park, Chiswick,
London W4 1JU,
England, U.K.
phone: 01-995-1868

Rex Peteet
ペティート，レックス

ノース・テキサス州立大学でデザインを勉強後、デザイン会社、広告代理店勤務。1982年ドン・シブレーとともに、シブレー／ペティートデザイン会社を創立。ダラス、ヒューストン、ロサンゼルス、ニューヨークのアートディレクターズクラブショウの年賞をはじめとして多くの賞を受賞。現在、ビジュアルデザイン、グラフィックデザイン団体の役員として活躍する他、大学やセミナーで講演もする。1985年、シブレー／ペティートデザイン会社では、ニューヨークADC賞6部門獲得。作品は『コミュニケーションアーツ』『プリントマガジン』『AIGA』『ニューヨークアートディレクターズショウ』(アメリカ)、『グラフィス』(スイス)などにとり上げられている。

Studied design at North Texas State University. Worked with several prestigious advertising and design firms including: The Bloom Agency, The Richards Group, Pirtle Design and Dennard Creative. In 1982 founded Sibley/Peteet Design Inc. with Don Sibley. At present member of the Dallas Society of Visual Communications, board of the Texas Chapter of the American Institute of Graphic Arts, co-chairman of the AIGA Texas Retrospective Show Committee and lecturer for various universities and art director/designer societies.
His work has been published in CA, New York Art Directors Show annuals, Print Magazine, Print Case Books, Graphis and AIGA design annuals. Two posters he designed, one for the opening of the Dallas Museum of Art and another for the IABC, were selected for the permanent collection of the Library of Congress.

Sibley/Peteet Design
2200 N. Lamar,
Suite 200, Dallas,
TX 75202, U.S.A.
phone: 214-954-1122

Keizo Matsui
松井桂三

1946年生まれ。大阪芸術大学を経て、84年松井桂三デザイン室設立。広告、パッケージ、グラフィック全般、商品企画開発、イメージ造成等、現在、クライアントは、国内、海外を問わず仕事の範囲は幅広い。78、79年、コミュニケーションアート展（アメリカ）優秀賞、80年パッケージング展部門賞、81年ニューヨークADC銀賞、83年大阪21世紀計画「築城400年祭」ポスター指名コンペ1席採用、84年ワルシャワ（ポーランド）、85年ラハティ（フィンランド）入賞、アフリカ自然保護ポスター展日本航空特別賞、86年ワルシャワポスタービエンナーレ入賞、パッケージング展部門賞、東京ADC賞、87年ミュンヘン近代美術館永久保存（ポスター4点）、ニューヨークADC入賞、パッケージデザインカウンシルインターナショナル（ニューヨーク）3点優秀賞、関西国際空港シンボルマーク指名コンペ1席採用。
ニューヨークADC会員、東京デザイナーズスペース会員、日本グラフィックデザイナー協会会員、日本パッケージデザイン協会会員。

㈲松井桂三デザイン室
〒540 大阪市東区内平野町
1-27 ベルボア501
phone 06-946-7612

Born in 1946, Graduated from Osaka University of Fine Arts and Music. 1984—Established Keizo Matsui & Associates engaged in advertisement, packaging, graphic design in general, product development and image conceptualization.
Awards: 1978, 1979—Award, Communication Art Exhibition, 1980—Award, Japan Package Design Association, 1981—Silver Medal, Art Directors Club, N.Y., 1983—1st Prize, Nominational Competition for Poster for Osaka 21st Century Plan, 1984—Award, International Poster Biennale, Warsaw, 1985—Award, Lahti Poster Biennale, JAL Special Prize for Nature Preservation in Africa Poster Show, 1986—Award, Japan Package Design Association, ADC Award (Tokyo), 1987—Award, ADC, New York, Award, Package Design Council International, 1st Prize, Nominational Competition for Symbol Mark for Kansai Airport.
Membership: Art Director's Club New York, Tokyo Designers' Space, Japan Graphic Designers' Association, Japan Package Design Association

Keizo Matsui and Associates
Belle Voix 501
1-27, Uchihiranomachi
Higashi-ku, Osaka 540,
Japan
phone: 06-946-7612

Takaaki Matsumoto
松本高明

1954年金沢市生まれ。74年渡米。79年アート・センター・カレッジ・オブ・デザイン卒業後、ギップス＆バルカインド社入社。82年ノル・インターナショナル社入社。87年マイケル・マッギンと共にM Plus M社をニューヨークで創立。現在、コミュニケーション・デザインとプロダクト・デザインを中心としたデザイン活動をニューヨークと東京で行う。ニューヨークADC銀賞、AIGAポスター／コミュニケーション／タイプ賞、ロサンゼルスADC賞、ニューヨーク・タイプ・ディレクターズ賞、CA賞、STA100賞、IDデザイン賞受賞。『グラフィス』(スイス)、『メトロポリス』(アメリカ)、『エフ・ピー』『ポートフォリオ』(日本)に掲載。

Born in Kanazawa in 1954. 1974—Moved to the U.S.A. 1979—Graduated from Art Center College of Design and employed by Gips & Balkind Associates. 1982—Employed by Knoll International, 1987—Established M Plus M in New York jointly with Michael McGinn. Presently involved in design activity centering on communications and product designs both in New York and Tokyo.
Awards: Silver Medal, New York Art Directors Show, AIGA Awards, Los Angeles ADC Award, New York Type Directors Award, CA Award, STA100 Award, ID Industrial Design Award

M Plus M
348 West 36th Street,
5-S, New York,
NY 10018, U.S.A.
phone: 212-629-5602

Ken Miki
三木 健

1955年神戸生まれ。74年片山デザインオフィス入社。82年三木健デザイン事務所設立。C.I.、B.I.、S.I.、パッケージ、エディトリアル、広告など、グラフィック全般の仕事に携わる。企業イメージから立体に至るまで、環境に関わっていく仕事に興味をもっている。

三木健デザイン事務所
〒530 大阪市北区天神橋
1-3-4 中之島フラッツ602
phone 06-358-5270

Born in Kobe in 1955. 1974—Graduated from Kobe Designer Gakuin, and employed by Katayama Design Office. 1982—Established Ken Miki Design Office for graphic design in general including corporate, brand and shop identity, package, editorial and advertisement. Currently extending his interest from corporate image to three-dimensional designs, all related with environment. Exhibition: 1980—"Love Stories of Fairies" Exhibition, Kyoto, "Picture Books Created from Dialogue" Exhibition, Osaka.

Ken Miki Design Office
Nakanoshima Flats 602,
1-3-4, Tenjinbashi,
Kita-ku, Osaka 530,
Japan
phone: 06-358-5270

Hiroshi Morishima
森島 紘

1944年東京生まれ。65年多摩美術大学卒業後、ロスアンゼルス・アートセンタースクール留学。70年ニューヨークCBS他に勤務。73年日本デザインセンター入社。80年タイム・スペース・アート設立、現在に至る。79年東京ADC賞、デザインフォーラム銅賞、81年デザインフォーラム銀賞、83年国井喜太郎産業工芸賞、85年東京ADC賞受賞。

タイム・スペース・アート㈱
〒106 東京都港区南麻布
3-17-14
phone 03-440-0444

Born in Tokyo in 1944. 1965—Graduated from Tama Art University and studied at Los Angeles Art Center School. 1970—Worked for CBS and others in the United States. 1973—Employed by Nippon Design Center. 1980—Established Time-Space-Art
Awards: 1979—Tokyo ADC Award, Bronze Medal of Design Forum, 1981 — Silver Medal, Design Forum, 1983—The Kunii Industrial Arts Award, 1985 — Tokyo ADC Award

Time-Space-Art Inc.
3-17-14, Minami Azabu,
Minato-ku, Tokyo 106
Japan
phone: 03-440-0444

Daniel Lori
ロリ，ダニエル

スイス、チューリッヒ生まれ。建築製図工、ならびにスイス最大の流通会社ミグロス社デザイン部でインテリア・デザインの製図工として働く。その後、4年制のインテリア・デザイン学校を卒業。1985年、サンフランシスコのアカデミー・オヴ・アーツの大学院を卒業。その後、ミラノでオリベッティ社デザイン部に勤務。86年、ロリ・デザインを設立。現在、ヨーロッパとアメリカで活躍。
ロリのデザイン哲学は、デザインは純粋に二次元的でも三次元的でもなければ、厳密な意味で技術的でも有機的でもないという点である。デザインは与えられたテーマに解答を出すまでに、いろいろ複雑な作業が交錯するものである。また、現代のデザインとは地球規模のものになったと感じている。

Born and raised in Zürich, Switzerland. Worked as an architectural draftsperson and an interior-architectural draftsperson for the Migros design department, entered the 4-year interior and industrial design program at the Schule für Gestaltung in Zürich and earned a B.F.A. degree. Worked for the design studio of Edgar Reinhard in Switzerland. 1983 — Joined the Masters program at the Academy of Art College in San Francisco, concentrated his studies in computer graphics and corporate image. 1985-received M.F.A., moved to Milan to work as a designer with Olivetti's Corporate Identity Department. 1986—Established Lori Design.
At present work for both European and American clients.
His philosophy on design is that it is never purely two or three-dimensional nor strictly technical or organic. He feels that design contains a complexity of different task interactions within an arrangement of given or imagined needs. Design today is no longer a local issue. Through the international trade of industrial knowledge as well as cultural exchanges design has become a global aspect.

Lori Design
634 Powell Street
San Francisco,
CA 94108, U.S.A.
phone: 415-989-7377

協力

株式会社アクシス
株式会社オリコミ
京王帝都電鉄株式会社
財団法人日本産業デザイン振興会
サントリー株式会社
株式会社資生堂
株式会社誠文堂新光社
ソニー株式会社
株式会社電通
図書印刷株式会社
株式会社ポップス
松下電器産業株式会社
株式会社リクルート

COOPERATORS

Axis Inc.
Orikomi Advertising Ltd.
Keio Teito Electric Railway Co., Ltd.
Japan Industrial Design Promotion Organization
Suntory Ltd.
Shiseido Co., Ltd.
Seibundo Shinkosha Publishing Co., Ltd.
Sony Corp.
Dentsu Inc.
Tosho Printing Co., Ltd.
Pops
Matsushita Electric Industrial Co., Ltd.
Recruit Co., Ltd.

編集後記
松井桂三

POSTSCRIPT
Keizo Matsui

三次元の世界を表現の手段とする事は、格別に新しくはない。アートの世界では早くから試みられていたし、日常のレベルではポップアップ式のグリーティングカードなどが古くから市販されている。しかし、アドバタイジングの分野にこだわると、国内国外を問わず収集作業が難航した。とにかく数が少ないのである。最近、各媒体に3Dグラフィックスの手法を使った作品が数々出現しているが、構造的に新しいアイデアがあるものとなると極端に少なくなる。本書はそんな現状から、さらに選び抜いてまとめあげた、この領域では初めての作品集である。

メッセージする、というアドバタイジングに必要な最低条件を満たした上で、作り手がいかに遊べるか、これが3Dグラフィックスの醍醐味であろう。たとえ作品としての斬新性があったとしても、メッセージが適切でなかったり、わかりにくかったり、作り手の自己満足に終始していては失格である。構造上のアイデアのユニークさ、表現レベルの高さ、受け手側に与えるインパクトの強さが三位一体となり、洗練された作品に仕上がることが重要なのである。

また個人的に3Dグラフィックスの魅力について言えば、平面から立体へと大きく変化し、また平面に戻る、このプロットが面白い。立体になった瞬間、大きなショックを受け手に与えながら、何くわぬ顔で平面に戻ってしまう構造が、幼い頃のイタズラにも似て、作り手の興をそそるのである。

しかし、3Dグラフィックスの発展にはコスト面、印刷技術工程等、制作面で解決すべき課題も多い。まだ発展途上分野といえるだろう。今後、才能を持ったクリエイターたちが果敢にチャレンジしていくだろうが、本書がそのきっかけとなれば幸いである。

最後にここに掲載させていただいた作家の方々、メッセージをお送りくださったエミリオ・アンバース、虎新一郎両氏にこの場を借りて厚く御礼を申しあげたい。

"Three-dimensional" is not a new expression. It has been popularly used in the world of art and pop-up greeting cards for quite a long time. However, in the field of advertisement, the works using such method is so few that collecting even samples was difficult. Although three-dimensional graphics have become to be increasingly used these days through diverse media, very few of them are made from an original idea. This book contains selected specimens from such limited sources.

How the creator can blend advertising design with playfulness after satisfying the primary purpose of message communication: this is the zest of three-dimensional graphics. Even if a work may be full of novelty as design, it fails as a communication medium if the client's message is not properly conveyed. Uniqueness of idea, high quality of expression, and impact to the audience should be integrated for a sophisticated design piece. I am charmed with the plot that a flat surface can be transformed into a three-dimensional object, retaining, at the same time, its original shape.

After giving a pleasant shock to an audience, momentarily, it becomes a solid figure, surrendering the place nonchalantly. Like recollecting childhood naughtiness, it incites the creator's intriguing mind.

There are, however, some factors in technical process including high printing and cutting costs that need to be cleared for further spread of three-dimensional graphics.

We hope this book will provide an impetus for talented creators to make challenging production. Finally, we express our heartfelt thanks to the contributors of the various works, and Mr. Emilio Ambasz and Shin'ichiro Tora for their essays.

3Dグラフィックス
THREE DIMENSIONAL GRAPHICS

責任編集	松井桂三
装幀・レイアウト	松井桂三
撮影	福田匡伸・青木 昇・近田和男
翻訳	林 千根
編集制作	石川信子
発行者	橋本周平
発行所	株式会社六耀社
	〒160 東京都新宿区新宿2-19-12
	静岡銀行ビル5F
	PHONE 03・354・4020 FAX 03・352・3106
	振替 東京2-58856
写植	大日本印刷株式会社
	有限会社スタジオエール
製版・印刷	大日本印刷株式会社
製本	大日本製本株式会社

©1987 by Rikuyo-sha Publishing, Inc.
Printed in Japan

ISBN4-89737-067-1 C3070